Bullying Ends Here

My Life

Tad Milmine

Quantity Sales Discounts

If you wish to purchase a bulk order of the book for things such as school and community groups, anti-bullying organizations or workplace orders, discounts are available. Please visit www.bullyingendshere.ca and contact us to learn more.

Library and Archives Canada Cataloguing in Publication

Milmine, Tad 1974
Bullying Ends Here - My Life / Tad Milmine

Includes bibliographic references. ISBN: 978-0-692-60684-1

Copyright © Tad Milmine All rights reserved

Self Published, Calgary, Canada

Second edition October 2016

Cover Page Photo Credits: Dan Freeman, TDFoto.ca

Dedicated to Jamie and Adrian.

Physically absent but always close to my heart.

Tad

Table of Contents

The intent of this book is to share my story, through my eyes, the way that I saw and remember it. It's my story of being bullied, neglected and my struggles with mental illness along with how I rose above it. I hope to inspire others in similar situations by sharing what I went through and how I persevered. Much of my story has been documented in the media around the world. The intent is to record the events in my life from MY perspective and is not to discredit anyone else. To that end, I have tried to omit names, locations and relationships where possible.

Foreword

Tad's story is one that I don't wish any child to have to go through, although he has come out of it with amazing strength and integrity. I hope that anyone who reads Tad's story will be able to take something out of it, and do something positive with their life.

To the readers, I would like to say that there is a light at the end of the tunnel, and anyone can accomplish anything they put their mind to.

To the kids, I would like to tell them that Tad knows what it's like to be bullied, and have the feeling that no one loves or cares about them. They're not alone. For one, Tad is always there to listen, and he cares about each and every one of the kids that email him.

To the parents, keep an open mind when your kids try to talk to you. It might seem like a small issue to you, but it could be very important and lifesaving to the child. Listening and being active in a child's life is so important, especially these days.

To the teachers, listen to the kids, and get them help if needed, whether it's getting in touch with the parents, or other agencies that might be able to help.

Tad is honest, funny, caring, giving, and most of all, sincere.

Tad's story needs to be heard, and I'm sure most people will be able to relate to some of the stories in the book, and become more aware of what's happening in the world today.

Debbie Schmidt, Tad's Mom
7 January, 2015

You Didn't Know
by Tad Milmine

You didn't know that when I was a little boy, I had a dream that I wanted to be a Police Officer so that I could help people.

You didn't know that when I was five years old, I was holding a pillow tightly over my head each night, waiting for the yelling to stop.

That in that same year my parents would divorce and that my Mom would be replaced by a woman who didn't like me.

You didn't know that by the age of ten I would be locked in a dungeon when I wasn't in school. That I would be alone, with no one to talk to or comfort me.

You didn't know that when you started to call me names, and physically harm me, that the demons inside my mind were causing me so much more pain than you ever could.

You didn't know that those very same demons would allow me to believe that I would never amount to anything, that I was useless and that no one would like me.

You didn't know that by the time I was sixteen years old I was struggling with mental illness after all of those hurtful words and actions you laid on me relentlessly.

You didn't know that when I was in my twenties, mental illness would get the better of me and that I would try to commit suicide because I wanted it all to end.

You didn't know that I would hold onto that dream of wanting to be a Police Officer since I was a little boy so that now I would help people.

You didn't know that I would grow up to be the person that people do like and love.

You didn't know that you were wrong!

Introduction

Hi!

Thanks for reading my book and for wanting to learn about my life through my eyes. I never would have thought that our paths would cross like this but I am very grateful.

Although my life hasn't always been that great, the truth is that my life is one worth living and it has a positive outcome. I don't share my story with you because I want to shame or embarrass anyone. I don't want you to read the book and feel angry. I want you to read the book and know that dreams really can come true no matter how bad things may seem at the time. I want you to know that no matter how dark some days may appear, that there are many more bright ones ahead. I want you to know that you are not alone in however you feel. I want you to know that I am always here for you.

Thank you again for taking the time to learn about my life and I wish you well.

Your friend, Tad

Tad at nine months

Tad at five years

My First Memories

March 12, 1974. That's the day that I was born. Apparently I was quite comfortable in Mom's belly because I took my time coming into this world. It seems that my memories begin when I was around five years old. I lived with my Mom, Dad and younger brother in a rented home. My parents worked hard to make ends meet to provide my brother and I all that they could. The house was rather large and was located on a huge property that backed onto the river. I was always told that I was not to go too far in the woods behind our house because of the river. It was such a good feeling having so much property to play and explore. There was a barn of some sort that might have been used for horses or some form of storage many years prior. When I was there, it was my refuge, where I kept my toys and would play when it was raining outside. It was like a giant fort. The frame was all dried out wood; so dry that it almost looked grey in colour. The roof was in shambles as it had been neglected for many years. It sure was enough for me.

I don't recall exploring in the forest very much. Not too sure why not, perhaps it was the fear of the river, but the barn was always enough for me. I liked to spend lots of time outside playing.

The house itself was an old stone structure with an enclosed front porch with its windows covered in plastic to keep in the warmth. The plastic would never be removed no matter the time of year. We never used the porch for entertaining; it was more of a storage area. Once we entered the front door, the house had such potential. The hardwood floors throughout were beautiful. The main floor had a kitchen which was located directly ahead once one walked in the front door. It then opened into a dining area where many parties would take place over the years. A small bathroom was off the dining area.

The living room was immediately to the right when we entered the house, a large room with furniture that was slowly falling apart. It was like the furniture was made of some sort of strong yarn. There were stripes, light in colour then accenting brown stripes throughout. The couch had many rips, tears and stains on it. There was a matching reclining chair as well but that was my Dad's. He loved to sit there. As we walked up the staircase to the upper level, it too was all hardwood.

The banister, steps and side trim were all beautiful. At the top of the stairs we had three rooms: a bathroom, which was to the left, the bedroom that I shared with my brother directly ahead and my parents' bedroom to the right. My bedroom is what I remember best because I spent much of my time in there playing and exploring. It was a huge room with lots of natural light from the window, a large closet and even a crawl space that had moth balls in it.

My brother and I had two single beds on opposite sides of the room from each other. It was not uncommon for us to take our toys and throw them out our bedroom window and onto the overhang from the level below. Not too sure why we did that since we could never get them back but I can still see them sitting there now as I write this. The door to our bedroom had no stop to it so the doorknob simply broke a hole through the wall itself. I was young and had little respect for the house. None of us did. It was a rental and it was old.

There was a basement but it was off limits for me. The rules were clear that I was not to go down to the basement as it was dangerous and simply not a place for children. There was a time that I was told that a man lived down there that was in a straight jacket but I don't know where that ever came into my memory. Probably a way to keep me from going down there. The fear of the basement was instilled in me at a young age.

As a young boy, I was always happy. I loved to play and be around my parents. I could see, however, as time went on that my parents weren't enjoying being around each other very much. I never understood it at the time but they were growing apart, arguing more and they tended to do things with me individually rather than together like it used to be. I had no idea how bad things were between them because they were still just my parents. I loved them both very much. At night I could hear them arguing long after I had gone to bed.

Sometimes the yelling got so loud that I would pull my pillow over my head and wish it all to stop. I remember the tears being absorbed by my pillow as they fell from my eyes. I wanted everyone to be happy.

One day while I was playing in the front yard, I saw a tow truck pull up in our driveway. It was a beautiful summer day with the sun shining. I was told later that the family vehicle was being repossessed and towed away. Although I didn't understand what was going on, I knew that was not a good thing. I knew that my parents weren't rich. They were doing the best they could. Dad worked at a local factory and Mom at a bar. Meals were often very simple with pasta or bacon and eggs. Many of those meals were eaten together while sitting in the living room gathered around the television.

Financially, the pressure on the both of them to make ends meet while also caring for two young boys must have been tough.

As the weeks and months wore on, the arguing wasn't just taking place at night, it was now all day and every day. Looking back I saw the signs, but as a child, I just didn't know what was going on. It's all so confusing, frightening and sad. I always thought that it was my fault for them arguing and would try to have them stop. Sometimes I would ask them to stop, while other times I would ask them to play with me. I tried anything I could to distract them.

It seemed that the only time they were getting along, in fact having fun, was when company came over. I can remember my parents having the best of parties. All of their friends would come over, gather around the dining table and play cards while drinking. Alcohol was a big thing growing up. I was always around it. It wasn't a bad thing, however, because any time alcohol was present, everyone seemed to like each other. When Billy Joel was played on the record player, I was always the happiest. There was something about his music that always had me dancing and laughing right along with the adults.

Even when everyone was partying, I was included. It was like I was just one of them. People would have me sit on their knee, want to play games with me or just tell me how cute I was. I loved it. Never was I cast aside or told to leave the adults alone. The parties would always go on into the wee hours of the next day but I never minded. I could fall asleep to the music and laughter without a problem. It was much better than the arguing and I knew, for that night at least, my parents were happy too.

Even at five years old, I always had a fascination for the Police. I don't know where it came from or when it started.

No one in my family was in law enforcement, no one spoke of it that I recall. It was just something that I was interested in. That interest would evolve into a passion in a short period of time. I think with my parents arguing so much now, I always thought a Police Officer could fix it. Having the thought that 'when I grow up, I want to help people', would last with me to this day. I used to have a matchbox police car (dinky cars as we used to call them) that I would have by my side every day. I would play with it from morning till night. I loved to pretend that I was a Police Officer driving that car around.

Because our house was sort of on the outskirts of town, there weren't many other houses that close to us. Directly across the street, there were two boys close in age with me so we would play a lot. More often than not, I would go to their house and play. I always enjoyed being there because their Dad had a model railroad in the basement. I was fascinated by this as I too seemed to love model trains. Trains and Police cars. I would spend hours just watching this train go in circles in their basement. Their Dad had it permanently setup so there were also small houses, people, animals and lights. I can only imagine how long it took to assemble it all. The two boys weren't as interested in it as I was but maybe it's because they saw it every day.

Those boys and I would play from morning till night if we could. We were always in their basement if the weather wasn't that great. I remember us using the two end tables on each side of their couch and putting blankets over each one. I would be the visitor and go from one to the other to say HI. Silly looking back on it now but it sure was fun back then.

I don't recall whatever happened to the boys as they seem to have just faded with time and memory. I don't recall ever saying goodbye, or seeing them move away. It's like they just disappeared. They were gone.

Tad fourteen years

Tad sixteen years

Divorce

Mom and Dad were really not getting along at all. They were yelling and arguing on a daily basis now. I felt like I was being tugged back and forth between the two because I didn't want to disappoint either of them. I loved them equally and I was in the middle. At that age, I wasn't thinking about something like a separation or divorce. I was only thinking that I wanted them to love each other again. I wanted them to get along and for us all to live happily ever after. Sadly this hope was not to be. It got to the point that I would try to hide, to keep my mind busy. This was one of the first times that I felt like I wanted to be invisible. This would be a feeling that would continue to grow with the years to come.

My world as I knew it was closing in on me. My happy family was falling apart. My parents were different now. The fighting was out of control. I was hoping that friends would come over and the alcohol would come out. That was always the fix. Even this wasn't working anymore as the friends seemed to stop coming and the alcohol would only make it all worse. Our family was drifting apart like a canoe floating away from a riverbank.

I would see my Mom crying after a loud argument. I didn't know what to do or how to make her feel better. I was stuck. If I was with Mom then Dad would say something to get my attention, making me feel bad. It was like I was taking sides. If I was with Dad then Mom would do something to make me feel the same way. I couldn't win no matter what direction I took.

Sometimes when they would argue, I too would be crying. Mom or Dad would see me standing there and tell me to go up to my room. I was so confused because now I felt like their arguing was all my fault and I was getting in the way. Telling me to go to my room, equivalent to 'go away', was new. They had never said such things to me before. Up to my room I would go. I would jump into my bed and pull that pillow over my head. I didn't want to hear the shouting and banging that went along with it. Things were getting much worse.

I can recall one night, very late, the screaming was out of control. I heard my Mom scream out, 'I'm leaving!'. The door slammed shut as the walls in the house shook. I couldn't pull that pillow over my head any tighter. It was like everything came to a halt for me. The house went silent and I knew that she had left. This was new though as I don't recall it having ever happened before. One minute there was the screaming, and the next it was the silence. The screaming meant that my parents were together, the silence meant they were apart. I didn't know what I wanted more.

I fell asleep with the tears streaming down my face and the boogers drying to the side of my nose. I had no idea what would happen now. Even at age five I felt like I should be 'careful what I wish for'. I wanted the screaming to stop. It stopped, but only with a consequence.

The next day, I remember being in the kitchen with my Dad. The phone rang and he was talking in a loud voice. Not really a mean voice, but a stern one. I knew it was my Mom on the phone. I heard him say 'You tell him' as he handed me the phone in his outstretched hand. It's like it was yesterday when I asked 'Mom, when are you coming home?' on the phone to her. She then told me in a quiet tone, her voice breaking ever so slightly, that she wasn't coming home anymore. My world crashed because I didn't know what this meant. Was this only for the day? For a week? Forever??

I was too afraid to ask any questions to either of them.

I almost didn't want to know the answer. It was simple what I wanted; I wanted them back together and to be a happy family again. What I wanted wasn't going to be asked however. It wasn't up to me. My opinion didn't count. My parents were now separated.

I could tell that my Dad was hurting as well. We were lucky to have his parents, my grandparents, living about ten blocks down the road. We spent more time at their place than we had in the past. Without the car, however, we had to walk. On those cold nights, that walk seemed to take forever.

'That Woman'

It wasn't long after the divorce that my Dad felt as though he had met the new woman of his dreams. They started dating and hanging out a lot but I didn't see her that much.

I kept to myself when I could. I was still only five or six years old and didn't understand where Mom had gone, let alone who this new person was. Before long, she moved into my house. Although I don't have a lot of memories of when she first moved in, I was never really fond of her. There was just something about her that I didn't like. It was more than just being upset that Mom was gone. It was something different.

Right from the start, 'that woman' and my Dad were fighting quite frequently and she had a very loud set of lungs on her! She could scream like I had never heard before. I never dared go near her, or Dad, when the screaming took place. Many times Dad would just gather my brother and I up and we would walk to my Grandparents down the road. Sometimes our walk was in the wee hours of the morning. I never understood that. It was our house. Why are we the ones leaving?

We would go to my Grandparents' house and stay there for several hours, or even the night, to allow 'that woman' time to calm down. We would then walk all the way back home and wait for it all to start again. The signs were there that Dad's new relationship wasn't working out but he kept with it anyhow. I would tremble when the screaming started.

There were times that she would be screaming about me. I will never understand how I played a role in this from their perspective but I always felt like it was my fault. Not an argument or fight went by without it feeling like it was me. Looking back, I can see how that was the beginning of me slowly changing from being that happy little boy to something much different.

Within a year or so of Dad and 'that woman' being together, we moved. The house I had grown up in was now in the past as we moved to another rented house, which was only a few blocks down from Grandma and Grandpa's. This was good for me because we were closer to them but I was really sad to say goodbye to the old house. It was where my memories of our family started. Those memories were fading away. As a little boy, the move reinforced that Mom wasn't coming home. I guess I always held out hope on that.

The new house was a two-level, red brick home; simple but tidy and well-kept. We still had a large backyard to play in and some neighbours on all sides of us. The house grew on me in the days leading up to moving there. It grew on me until we moved in, that is. Upon moving into the new house, I learned that there was a basement. Just a large open space where the laundry machines and such would be. Your typical cement-walled, concrete floor basement. I thought nothing of it because I was already afraid of basements due to what I was told about our last one. Since I was old enough to walk, I was told that basements were off limits.

My bedroom was on the top floor of the house, directly across from Dad and 'that woman's'. The floors were hardwood and the stairway down to the main level of the home was between our bedroom doors. You couldn't walk anywhere in that house without the floors creaking, especially the staircase. The stairs curved towards the bottom and led to the only washroom in the residence. The main floor had a kitchen and living room along with a small bedroom that we used for storage.

Much of our time was spent in the living room when we first moved in. The screaming between those two continued to escalate in time and, one night while they were screaming, 'that woman' told me to go to the basement. Not only was I told to 'go away' but now I was told to go to a place that I feared the most: the basement! I was so confused and afraid at the same time. She was screaming so loudly that I could see how red she got in the face. Dad would mostly just sit there with a rum and coke in his hand. He was always so calm. He didn't scream at her much, not like he had with Mom.

In the middle of her screaming, she turned to look at me, with her red face and all and I was petrified. The look of fear was in her eyes. I quickly turned and opened the door to the basement and walked down the set of stairs directly in front of me. The stairs went down about eight steps and then they turned left or right for the final two steps. Both directions led to the same place. There was nothing in the basement for a child; no toys, just a grungy, dark and cold basement. I sat there and listened while I could hear the fierce fighting going on upstairs. I could tell that Dad was angry now also.

Having nothing to do, and being so afraid of the basement, I snuck up the steps, one at a time, and peeked through the crack of the door jamb. I could see they were both in the kitchen now and she was relentless. They just kept screaming. Dad was useless and not doing anything while I was now in the basement, a place I was never allowed to be until now. I was a scared child, lost in what to do. I had nowhere to turn. I sat there with my heart pounding while I peeked through the crack in the door. Whenever she came towards the door, I would race down as quickly as possible so that she wouldn't know that I was up there, listening to them.

Dad called for me to come upstairs at some point and told me to grab my coat. I knew we were going to Grandma and Grandpa's again. I got my winter coat off of the hook and put on my boots. She continued to scream at Dad as I rushed to get ready. She then turned her screams towards me, yelling things like, 'Oh sure, take that little suck with you!' and 'Get the hell out of here, both of you!'. I just wanted Dad to hurry up so we could get out. I was hoping that maybe this would be the time that he would leave her. We walked the few blocks to my Grandparents' house as the cycle began again.

Grandma would cuddle with me and tell me how much she loved me while Dad would get a drink and sit in the kitchen smiling at me. The sadness in his eyes was there.

My Grandma was always so proud of me. I can still remember her taking me to the local department store when I was just a young child. We wanted to go to the lower level but had to take an escalator. I had never seen one before. I remember she stretched her wrinkled hand out to me, gave me the look of 'trust me' and held me tight as I stepped onto the first stair. She would do the same thing for my first time on a city bus. One of my favourite memories with Grandma was when she made her roast beef dinners on Sunday nights. Walking into her house on those days was incredible. The smells of the roast, homemade gravy and the creamed corn would linger in the air. She was an amazing woman.

Grandpa had been in the war and typically always stayed in the back living room. He had mobility issues and he drank a lot. It was also hard for him to speak. Sometimes it was from alcohol but it was also from his disability. His words were always garbled up and difficult to understand. Grandpa and I had a bond that was very special to me. Typically we wouldn't say much but I always gave him loads of hugs and spent time with him watching TV. One of the shows we would watch together was T. J. Hooker. This was our favourite Police show, which I cherished. I was watching it with my Grandpa. I think I was the only person in the family that ever made it a point to spend time with him.

Dad loved to play baseball and would go a couple of times per week. I loved those days because 'that woman' hated baseball. She would never go so it was quality time with my Dad. He loved having me there. I could feel it. He would throw the ball around with me before a game and also let me be the bat boy during the game. He would tell me when I could run out and grab the bat the previous batter had just used. I felt so important and wanted. It was a break for us from 'that woman'.

Dad was an entirely different person when he was with his friends at baseball. He was the life of the party. Everyone loved my Dad because there was so much laughing and partying. It wasn't uncommon for us all to meet at a local pub after the game and sit and laugh together. Dad made it a point to include me. He never pushed me away or asked me to be quiet. He would give me some change to play video games or introduce me to some of the other kids that were there. Those were some of my best times growing up.

One particular day after playing a baseball game, the team got together for some drinks. It was a Sunday afternoon and everyone was having a great time. 'That woman' figured out where we were and started calling the house ordering us to come home. Dad knew that was not good news but he continued to drink and just tell her that we would leave soon. It felt like hours before we finally did get home but, when we did, it was World War Three. We walked in the back door and she started screaming immediately. The fun was over.

The look on her face was beyond fury. I was terrified. I had never felt that way before. Something had changed again!

As I walked in the back door, her anger was directed at Dad but I was physically between them, in the middle of the hallway. She was screaming about how she had been expecting us hours ago and how she had made dinner which had now spoiled. She took the pot from the stove and walked towards me. She was screaming how everything was ruined and then dumped the contents of the pot right over my head. An entire pot of macaroni and cheese was now being dumped all over me. Bit by bit, each piece of pasta was falling off the side of my head. Some got stuck in my hair, other pieces in my clothing. The rest on the floor. Dad yelled for me to go to the basement. The first time he had ever told me that. I ran!

I then heard him scream and a lot of curse words were exchanged. I knew the fight was now physical as he was trying to stop her from hitting him and throwing things around. Dad finally had enough and reached for the phone, which was on the wall at the top of the basement stairs. Right in view of my sitting spot that I used to peek through the door. I could see him grab the phone and dial a number as he told her that he was calling her parents. Enough was enough.

She went into an even greater rage and ran to the phone.

They physically pushed and shoved each other but I could tell Dad had someone on the line because he was talking to someone other than 'that woman'. As he was talking on the phone, using his other arm to keep her back, she continued to scream. She then grabbed the phone and simply pulled it right off the wall. The line went dead. The phone sat in pieces on the floor along with bits of the wall and plaster.

'That woman's' parents only lived a few kilometers

away and they drove over. I heard them come in the front door and I could tell that everyone was shouting but that her parents were working to calm her down. They all went to the spare room on the main floor and everyone slowly calmed down. No one came to me. I was forgotten about in the basement. I was still in shock and horrified at what had happened with the pasta. I was now petrified of 'that woman' and that feeling would never leave me.

He wasn't going to be allowed to play baseball for much longer. 'That woman' was going to have no part of that!

Mom had some visitation rights. I don't know if they were sorted out through the courts or through mutual understanding between her and my Dad but the agreement was that I could go with her every Saturday night at 7pm through until Sunday night at 7pm. I used to get so excited to go with her as it was a form of escape along with getting to see her. Solid Gold was a TV show that was on Saturday nights from 6pm to 7pm so I would sit at the front door waiting for Mom. 'That woman' and Dad would be in the living room beside the front door watching the show.

It wasn't uncommon that Mom wouldn't show up to get me. Without the use of cell phones and such back then, she just wouldn't come. 'That woman' loved when she could tell me how even my Mom didn't love me and would yell at me to get back to the basement. I was at a loss. What happened to Mom? Why didn't she save me? The basement was gradually becoming the place that I had to be. As much as I was afraid to be down there, it was a reprieve to be away from 'that woman'.

On the nights that Mom would come and get me, we had a great time. She was working in bars and pubs and of course, Saturday nights were her busy nights. She would give me a huge hug and kiss and then drop me off at a babysitters for a few hours while she worked. She would then wake me up sometime around two or three in the morning, bundle me up in my winter coat as I was still half asleep, and drive me to her apartment. We made the best of our times together.

One thing that 'that woman' was not going to permit was for me to spend any time with my Mom's parents. I barely have any memories of them. I just didn't see them that often. The memories that I do have I hold close to my heart.

The only room in this house that I felt safe in was my bedroom. In fact, I would be there as much as possible to avoid her. Because the washroom was on the main level, where she would be, I would pee out of my window. I avoided her at all cost. With the steps always creaking so much, I couldn't even sneak down. She was always angry at me and I was crying more and more. I was so afraid. I was living in constant fear of her unpredictable mood swings.

We didn't live in that red brick home for very long. Perhaps a year or so. We were then moving to another house but this one would be across town and much farther away from my Grandparents. This new house would also have a basement. A dark, musky and frightening basement.

The Basement

The move to the new house meant a change in schools. I was eight years old when we moved. The new house was across town from my grandparents with a large river separating us. Although the move was an improvement compared to where we lived prior, it was hard to be so far away from my grandparents. They were my support and were always just a walk away. They protected me and I always felt safe with them. I would never be able to just walk to their place. It felt like we had moved across the Country. I wasn't safe anymore.

The new house was beautiful. It was dark grey in colour with a stucco finish, with very nice landscaping and plenty of garden space. It had a large back yard, big wooden garage to match the colour of the house and a long driveway. The new house was also three stories if one counts the basement. One of the nicest parts of it was the large front porch. With the slight slope up to the front of the house, it was like our house towered over the others in the area. I remember Dad and 'that woman' doing a lot of work on the new house prior to us moving in. By the time I saw the place, everyone was excited for the move, including me. I didn't have any friends that I was leaving behind and I only had bad memories of the old house so I was thinking the new house would be a fresh start. I couldn't have been more wrong.

As soon as we moved into the new house, it was painfully

clear that the basement was going to be where I spent my time. I was told right away that I would have my own 'play area' down there. The basement however was very dark, wide open, cold and had a musky smell to it. When we walked down the five steps from the main floor level, one would find the side door to the house. A sharp turn to the right and there were another five steps to the basement. The bottom five steps were open underneath and I was always afraid someone would reach through and grab my ankles as I walked down.

I don't know where that fear came from but it stayed with me for years. I would jump down as many steps as I could to prevent that from happening.

The walls were a light coloured cement. Parts that wall were slowly falling apart with bits of stone laying beneath them. The floor was also cement and painted chocolate brown. There was no heat or air conditioning in the summer and it always had a terrible chill to it in the winter. The basement was designed to be for laundry, excess storage and the furnace area but, now that we lived there, it would be for so much more. With one window being cemented over, another broken and the last two covered over on the outside, I was never able to see out. I was given a small fabric couch with reds and browns in the fabric. A small wooden table would be used for my feet to keep them off the cold floor and I was given a small black and white television. Of course this was long before DVD players, video gaming systems or computers were invented. Needless to say, there was not a lot of entertainment for me.

It became very clear in a short period of time that I was going to spend a lot of time in the basement, in fact, it would be all of my time.

The door at the top of the stairs was a simple wooden

door. It opened up into the kitchen on the main floor. The main level of the home had a living room and family room as well, however, I would rarely ever see these rooms. The steps to go up to the top floor were by the front door and they rounded as you went higher until you reached the three bedrooms and only bathroom in the house. My bedroom was at the top of the steps on the immediate left. Just a very tiny room at that. I had barely enough room for a single bed, lamp stand and small desk. My little closet had a sloped ceiling and a few shelves for clothing. I think this room might have been used for a small sitting room prior to us moving in; certainly not a bedroom.

I don't recall how it all began with me being forced to stay in the basement but I know it was from the moment we moved into that house. I was told right away that there was 'no need for kids upstairs'. She would tell me this over and over until I actually started to believe that. My Dad would never say anything. He would just stand there with his rum and coke in hand and allow her to make the rules. She was in control and no one was going to change that. Dad was turning to alcohol a lot more now.

When we first moved in, I would be called upstairs for dinner typically around 5pm. I would sit at the table and not say a word while eating my dinner. It was always an awkward silence with us. I wouldn't dare say anything for fear that she would yell at me. I was so afraid. I always was afraid when I was around her. The abuse was getting worse though. I could feel it from within. I was starting to cry more and more and always looked at the ground. I was afraid that she would see me and I figured that if I kept my head down, she wouldn't see me. I would be invisible. I just wanted to be invisible. In the years ahead, my time at the dinner table would fade as 'that woman' would decide which nights she wanted me with the rest of the family. The meals she didn't want me up stairs for, I would eat my dinner off the floor by myself at the top of the steps and only five minutes to eat as much as I could. It just became that way for me.

When dinner was over, I had to clean up and do the dishes by hand. Dad and 'that woman' would go into the living room and watch TV. I would always hope that they hadn't cleaned off the plates yet so that I could find food scraps to get me through the night. More often than not, I was able to find something, if not from a plate then from the garbage can.

They had cable television, unlike myself. When I was done my chores I would immediately go back downstairs, careful to always close the door behind me, and sit on the couch. With the chill always in the air, I would typically curl up in the corner as tight as I could to stay warm. I would watch CBC television through the fuzz on the TV as I only had antenna.

I would sit in that basement, for hours on end, dreaming. I would make up silly games in my head to help pass time. I would imagine what life would be like if Mom would come back. I would wish that someone would come and save me. With the basement ceiling only being the wooden frame, I could hear everything down there. To this day, the most frightening sound for me was always when the floorboards creaked. When that happened, I knew that someone was moving about and I would hold my breath hoping it wasn't her. I always knew who was walking by how heavy the footsteps were. I could tell where they were going and exactly where they were upstairs. I was hyper-sensitive to sound down there. My anxiety would spike and recede by the minute. My greatest fear was always when I would hear her up and moving and then the basement door opening up.

I knew she was coming downstairs. I hated that creaking sound. It triggered such fear in me, that I could feel the tingling of apprehension and dread, because I instinctively knew her abusive routine.

Perhaps she would come down to put a load of laundry in the washer or to fold the clothes from the dryer. Sometimes it was a quick visit to take something out of the freezer. Sometimes it was to come and speak to me. The fact that the basement was so open left me little place to hide and be invisible. She would always look over at me every time she came down there. No matter how nice I tried to be, or even if I never said anything at all, she always had something to say. This is how it always started.

She would give me some order or command to do something. I would simply agree and do it. I would never dare stand up to her and say something, or refuse to do what she was telling me. With my anxiety at its highest peak when she was down there, and we were alone, I would just break down crying.

I would try so hard to hold it in, to fight it off, but I could never do it.

She would see or hear me crying and start to laugh. It wasn't long before the names started like 'cry baby'. She would always be so sharp with me telling me to stop crying. It wasn't like I could just stop. It wasn't something that I could control. I just wanted those moments to end so I could be left alone to wait it out. It was humiliating and I knew that I was so vulnerable. I always thought that something was wrong with me. When she would go back up the stairs and I would hear the door slam shut, I would relax a bit. This is how my average day went. If she happened to have yelled loud enough at me, Dad would come down afterwards to see what she said. He wouldn't do anything about it but it was comforting to have him come down. He would give me a hug, tell me to ignore her, and disappear up the steps until I heard the door click shut. He never slammed the door.

I can't tell you how many times Dad told me to 'ignore her'. Hundreds? Thousands perhaps. Over and over he would come to the little boy and tell me to ignore her. He never did what he simply should have which was talking to her. I think he too was afraid of her. We were now in a house where a creak of a floorboard would frighten me. Where I would cry uncontrollably and where I would be confined.

I recall on a couple of occasions hearing a knock at the front door upstairs and hearing the footsteps head in that direction. I could hear everything in the basement and would recognize voices. It was my Mom's parents asking to see me briefly to give me something that Grandma had knitted. I would hear the door slam shut and I would never receive what she wanted me to have. Heartbreaking really. What makes it worse is that shortly after my last memory of the door slamming on them, is that I would never see them again. One morning when I was around eleven or twelve years old, I had woken up and gotten ready for school. I headed down the stairs where she was standing and waiting for me. I stopped in my tracks. This was not the normal routine. Something was up. She looked at me with a stern look on her face and said, 'Tad, your Grandparents were killed in a car crash last night'. That was it. She walked away. No one would ever sit me down and explain what death was, I wasn't allowed to go to the funeral and I was expected to go to school as usual that day. I often wonder what it would have been like to have had them in my life. I still go to their grave each time I am back in Ontario to say Hi and talk to them a bit. It's important to me. I learned later that they had been struck by a drunk driver and passed at the scene.

That door at the top of the stairs would be something I would fear for years. I knew there was a lock on the other side too. Just a small little latch lock that would break with the slightest of force used, but I would never dare. It always felt to me like that door was as strong as a vault door. It was never to be opened. I was already afraid of basements and now I was put in this one with very little to do and no escape. I was so afraid of that door. As much as I was fearful of her coming downstairs, it was equally frightening for me to go up. I would do anything I could to never have to go up there. Unfortunately, there were many times in a day that I had no choice. With only one bathroom in the house, on the top floor none the less, I couldn't avoid her forever.

Even when I had to simply use the washroom, I would have to knock on the door at the top of the steps and wait. I would wait for her voice to say, 'WHAT?'. Only then could I ask permission to use the washroom. Once she said yes, I would have to open the door so gently because I never knew if the lock was on or not. If it opened then I would run up and through the kitchen so quickly so I wouldn't see her. The same again on the way down ensuring I always closed the door behind me. I would get so afraid of her that I would eventually use the drain in the laundry sink to go to the washroom. That saved me the anxiety, as gross as that was.

The taps for the laundry machine would be where I would get a drink. I would unhook the laundry machine from the valve, cup my hands and drink. Once I was done I was careful to hook it all up again nice and tight. That was a secret that I never told anyone growing up. I certainly didn't want her knowing so that she could tighten the tap so I couldn't use it anymore.

There really wasn't much for me to do down there. I did become a big fan of the Toronto Blue Jays at a young age though because the only channel I really got on my TV was CBC which used to carry the games. That would occupy many hours for me each day and I would analyze everything about the team. I would keep daily statistics on each game and player. I would keep it all written down in a binder I created each year and learn all that I could. It was like I was in the game itself when it was on. I was in the zone and it took my thoughts to a positive place for the time being. I was able to sneak a tennis ball in one day and would hide it in the drain pipe in the floor. I would throw this ball against the cement wall hundreds of times a day. I would pick a point on the wall to hit and worked on my aim that way. Of course I couldn't do this anytime I wanted because of the sounds but I was very careful to do it when I was safe. I can't imagine what would happen if she knew I was doing that.

For Christmas one year, I was given a model railroad set. This was huge for me because holidays were never really a special time of year for me. Gifts were always articles of clothing. Not exactly the item a child wants for Christmas! I used the toy railroad on a daily basis in the basement. I would always be changing up the layout or moving the cars around on the tracks. It was set up on the floor in the far corner of the basement. I knew this was not something she liked because toys were not an item she ever approved of for me down there. I was sure to keep it tidied up when I wasn't using it. I wanted the train to also be invisible so she wouldn't take it away from me. After a couple of years, she did just that.

While every holiday was just another day to me, Christmas was a little bit different. Not because of the magic of the season or for the gifts I would (or wouldn't) get, it was because I could leave the basement on Christmas Eve night with 'that woman's' Stepdad. He was allowed to take me to church with him and we would sing carols. Although I was never a religious person, I always enjoyed any opportunity I could to get out. After church, we would go to his house and sit by the fire while eating meatballs and other snacks. At some point Dad and 'that woman' would come over as well and I would be sent to bed. She wanted nothing to do with me being upstairs and around everyone. Sending me to bed was the quickest solution and Dad would never say a word. Even writing this I am floored that no one caught on to what was going on with her abuse.

I don't recall ever seeing Mom during the holiday season. I am not sure if she wasn't allowed or maybe with work it wasn't possible. As for Grandma and Grandpa, only Dad and I would go over first thing in the morning on Christmas day for a short visit. We would exchange gifts and then head back to the house. 'That woman' would never go to their house.

Of course that was just fine by me. More time alone with Dad. With Grandma and Grandpa being on a very strict budget and not having much money, our gifts were always very basic. That was certainly fine by me as the holiday itself wasn't special to me, only the fact that I got to be with them. Aside from an artificial Christmas tree that Grandma would setup in the front room of their house, I don't recall any decorations at all.

Once a year, typically in the summer, 'that woman's' Stepdad was allowed to take me out for one day. He was the nicest of men. I always felt as though he cared when I was with him. Everyone loved him as his personality was contagious. Always laughing and smiling, he would walk with his arm around me, so proud to have me there. He would always ask me where I wanted to go. I was empowered to make a decision of such great proportions. One of my favourite times of the year by far. He and I went to Canada's

Wonderland several times. The rides, the fun, the carnival smells and hearing everyone having such a great time was magical. For a short while, I felt just like everyone else.

One year, he took me to Detroit, Michigan for my first trip to the United States. It was like an entirely different world to me. I remember being in the car while we drove across the bridge separating the two Countries and he put Bruce Springsteen's 'Born In The USA' tape on. He and I both sang so loudly together while we drove. I was in heaven. These yearly trips would last until I was seventeen years old.

As we got more settled in the new house, Dad wanted a fridge in the basement to keep his beer and Diet Coke cold. They set one up one evening while I stayed in my own area. Of course I could see all that they were doing but I stayed clear of her. At some point, Dad called me over to where they were by the fridge. He looked at me and asked me to get a beer for him. It was really weird because he was standing right there so why would I need to get the beer for him? I hesitated having no idea what was going to happen. I reached for the fridge thinking something was going to jump out at me or perhaps fall out. I was wrong because as soon as I touched the fridge handle, I got a strong shock, because the fridge hadn't been grounded. They both cracked up laughing and I was mortified. For the first time, my Dad had just done something so cruel. I felt abandoned like I lost my only ally. To this day, I hesitate when opening fridges. Dad really let me down that day and I have never forgotten that incident.

When the baseball game wasn't on TV, or when my arm was too sore to throw the tennis ball anymore, I would be curled up on the couch dreaming of what life would be like without her in it. My dreams always seemed to include me being a Police Officer.

More and more as the years went on, that was all that I

could think about. Perhaps it was my time with Grandpa watching T. J. Hooker, or maybe a school visit from an Officer, I just always wanted to be one. I would hear a siren outside and wish I could see them speed past. I would wonder where they were going, what would they do when they got there. I always knew that someone was calling them for help and they were rushing off to do just that. I wanted to help also. First though, I would be the one who needed the help.

The basement was where I spent most of my time growing up. Aside from the odd day trip I was allowed, or to visit Grandma and Grandpa, I was not permitted to leave the basement....unless I went to school.

This is the door that enters into the kitchen/ living room upstairs. This door was like a vault to me and I don't remember a single time of turning that knob without my heart pounding out of my chest. This is also where 'that woman' stood and screamed down at me.

There were always shoes at the bottom of the stairs. We used to have an orange carpet covering each stair. The window on the left, with the crumbling paint, is exactly as it was when we lived there.

This is the sink that I used as a toilet and also the taps where I would sneak a drink of water by disconnecting the laundry machine connections.

The fridge was right below the window and my area was to the right of that.

This is the area that I used to sit in. The stuff you see here is from the current owners who were kind enough to take photos to help give an idea of what the basement physically looked like in the past. The light you see was the only one I had when I was in the basement.

This is the door I walked out of when I left home. To the right is the lower part of the stairs leading to the basement.

Sexual Abuse

*B*efore my grandparents passed away, they were placed in a retirement home. This was much better for Grandpa as his mobility wasn't there and Grandma simply couldn't do everything for him anymore. With the available care, they were well cared for. The retirement home was a good twenty minute drive from our house so we weren't going to see them as often. It was typically only on Sundays that we would go and visit them. Of course 'that woman' would never go with us as she never really did like them. I really can't remember anytime that she went to see them, whether it be at their house or at the retirement home.

Dad always gave me a choice to go or not on Sundays to visit. Of course I wasn't going to stay at home alone with 'that woman' and I wanted to see my Grandparents badly. They were so important to me. We would go up and sit in their room and share stories. Grandma's health was failing quickly as she was having heart attacks frequently. Her memory was fading and it would take time for her to remember who I was at times. I got used to it and never took it personally. I knew that she was just happy to have company. She would smile from ear to ear and always tell everyone that I had her nose. Towards the end, she was forgetting my name and who I was, but I always had her nose.

Grandpa would pass before Grandma did. I remember that last time I saw him, he smiled and gave me a hug. His fingers were all curled up and he was unable to do much on his own. I helped him into his wheelchair and took him for a walk. The retirement home was quite long and curved so we would walk as far as we could and I would do that talking. I could never really understand him, and I think he knew that also, so we would just smile at each other while I spoke. It was heartbreaking to see.

With Grandma's health being as bad as it was, she was moved to a different wing in the retirement home once Grandpa passed. Our visits with her were much shorter given the more intense care that was required. We would visit briefly and say hello. She was unable to speak much and was always very tired. The woman who introduced me to so much, who was my safety blanket and whom I loved beyond words was now a very fragile woman who could barely speak. I can still remember her smile as I write this.

With our visits now much shorter at the retirement home, Dad and I would go to visit a family friend who lived nearby. They had a son who was several years older than I was so he and I would always go play elsewhere while the adults visited. I didn't mind this at first because it was like a breath of fresh air for me. More often than not we would go to their basement but it was nothing like mine.

Theirs was furnished with a games room, TV room and a spare bedroom. It wasn't a negative thing to go down there. Plus I knew that Dad would be enjoying the time out as well.

Their son wasn't always there when we went over but when he was, it was fun to hang out at first. We would play ping pong, hide and seek or video games. There always seemed to be something fun to do there. I can remember one day that things between us changed. We were sitting on a couch and he started talking about girls. I was only about nine years old at the time and didn't really understand what he was talking about. I really enjoyed our time together, and the companionship, so I would listen intently. As he kept talking about girls, I felt his hand reach over and grab my right knee. I wasn't sure why he did this but he just left it there while he was still talking.

As he continued with his stories, his hand continued to move up my leg to my inner thigh. I was very uncomfortable and confused as I had no idea what was happening. I didn't know what to say or even how to say it. I was frozen. That was the first time the abuse took place. I can only describe it as confusion and terror all in one. I was so afraid to disappoint him by pushing him away or saying, 'NO' because my life was full of dislike and disappointment. It seemed like everyone hated me or I was making them mad. My only friend was now physically hurting me and I had no idea what to do.

Right away, I knew one thing for sure, it was that I wasn't going to tell anyone.

I was ashamed and felt dirty. When it was over, I felt like a zombie. He kept talking to me like nothing had happened and whatever took place, that it was perfectly normal. I had no idea what 'normal' in life was supposed to be like but I knew this wasn't it. I was very quiet and reserved. I had no idea what to say from that point on. It felt like an eternity before Dad called down the stairs telling me it was time to go. I just got up and ran up the stairs. The car ride home was very quiet as my anxiety was high having just experienced what I did while now realizing that I am going back home.

Our visits to that house would continue. I always had the choice on whether to go or not. My options were simple; be home alone with 'that woman' or go to that family's house and be sexually abused. I always chose to go to that house. I could not bear the thought of being alone with 'that woman'.

Every time we went to that house, I always hoped that he wouldn't be there. Sometimes I would get lucky and he wouldn't be home, or he would sleep the entire time we visited. Those times were alright because I got to sit with my Dad. The other times were terrible. As soon as he would come into the living room where we were, we were directed to go play and hang out. I always knew what that meant.

Each time we met, things would happen quicker and be more severe. I would just revert to being a zombie and lay there. I never pushed him away, I just couldn't. He was much older and bigger than I was plus I was so afraid to upset anyone else in life. I just put up with it.

No matter how much it hurt, I just cooperated with him. I would try to take my mind somewhere else which was always a challenge because I didn't have many places to take it. I never had much experience with life outside the basement. I would always try to focus on my dream about being a Police Officer. I would focus so hard on those thoughts just to not know what was happening to my body. It was like I was separate from it. I would still hear him talking while he was abusing me. He would always talk like nothing was going on. I don't think I can ever explain the emotions that were running through my mind. I didn't know it was abuse until much later in life. I didn't even know if what was going on was normal or not. I just knew that I didn't like it and that I had no choice.

From an adult's perspective, they always would have thought we were having a great time, just being quiet in the basement. I know they had no idea what was going on. My abuser would do what he could to make it look like we were playing before he got started on me. I know of a few times that I can think of that we would go downstairs and use the ping pong table for a game of house. He would fold the table up and slide a blanket down the middle to divide the underside into 'houses' and then put blankets all around the table to keep the two 'houses' concealed. He would take cans of food from their pantry area and put them inside each 'house'. He would then come to 'visit' my 'house' and the abuse would start all over again. If an adult ever were to come down, it would look perfectly normal to them and we were hidden from plain sight.

I can tell you that it never crossed my mind to tell anyone. It simply wasn't an option for me. Although this abuse would take place on and off for several years, I always chose to go to his house. I was simply too afraid to be alone with 'that woman' and I also wanted to be with my Dad. I always felt safe with him. I don't blame him for what happened to me at that house because I know the abuse was well hidden. To this day, I know that he would never have known. No one did. There are only two people that know what happened and I still struggle with it.

I don't know why our visits there ended but we just stopped going. Dad was not playing baseball anymore and I always blamed 'that woman' for it. I know that Dad loved the sport very much and had the best of friends there. She would never go to any games and certainly didn't like when he played or went out with the guys afterwards. Now with my Grandparents gone and baseball over, I wouldn't be leaving that basement very much now.

Dad got pretty creative with a nightly ritual for us as time went on. Typically, 'that woman' would go to bed around 8pm or so. I always knew the time based on the shows on CBC TV and I would wait for her footsteps to be heard on the creaking floorboards. I would hear her steps lead to the bottom of the stairs to the upper floor and then, one by one, the steps would creak until she got to the top. I would sit in the basement with the TV turned down real low and wait. After about ten minutes or so, I would hear Dad get up from the couch and slowly walk to the top of the basement steps.

I would hear the door being opened and his voice would softly say, 'OK, you can come up now'. It was like he was telling me the coast was clear and inviting me to be a normal human being for a short while.

I would go up and sit on the same couch as he did. I never sat on her couch. He would lay down and put his legs over my lap and cover us both up with the afghan blanket. It was my time to spend with Dad. We never really spoke much. I assume that was because we were afraid that she might hear us. With their bedroom being right above the living room, Dad and I could always hear if she was getting up and that would give me a few seconds to spring up and race to the basement door. We had quite a few close calls over the years. At 9pm I would head up to my room just like the rules stated. Dad would always give me a hug and kiss and we would tell each other how much we loved one another.

I was consistently very careful to walk up the stairs to the bedroom area very quietly, as to not wake or stir 'that woman'. It was like walking on eggshells all the way up to my room. I would close my bedroom door ever so slowly so she wouldn't hear the click of the clasp. It was a very slow process to get the door closed quietly but it was important that I did it right. It wasn't worth the fear of her waking up or knowing I was there. I never knew if she would have one last thing to yell at me about, how noisy I had been.

In bed I would put my alarm clock on silent mode and use my headphones to listen to CHYM FM's top 5 at 9. Back then it was my way of knowing the day was over and I was safe for a few hours. I would lay in bed hearing the songs and hearing how each one would stay on the charts for a certain period of time while I would look out my window and watch the kids outside playing. I would open my bedroom window and smell the fresh air and just watch. It was interesting to watch how the kids were laughing and free to come and go as they wanted. They would throw balls around, play badminton or ride their bikes around. In the summer, it would still be light outside until 10pm so I had lots to watch.

The songs that were on the top five back then still come on the classic 80's channels from time to time now. I find myself changing the channel quickly as they bring me right back to those memories of laying in bed watching the kids while being fearful of waking 'that woman' who was only a few feet away from me. I would drift off to sleep and dream of being a Police Officer.

School

My first memories of school would be the start of grade three. I recall being very shy and introverted and not really knowing what to say to others around me. My parents had been apart for a few years and now 'that woman' had moved in and created a lot of anxiety in my little mind. It was part way through this school year that I was going to be moved to a new school as we had moved across town.

The first day in the new school was part way through the year so I had to adjust quickly. I remember the terrible feeling of walking into the classroom where everyone had been sitting on the floor looking at the teacher who was writing on the chalk board. When I was walked into the class by the school Secretary, everyone turned to look at me. The teacher was lovely. In her very soft and welcoming voice she came up and introduced herself to me. Miss McPherson was her name and I will never forget it. She had long black hair and a beautiful smile. She then turned, put her arm around me, and introduced me to the class. I went from being so afraid when I walked into the class, to feeling very comfortable with her arm around me. She certainly made the experience of being new much easier.

As much as I enjoyed her, I never made any quality friends at school. I was just too afraid and reserved. I couldn't even say 'HI' if someone came up to me. I know this had to do with the neglect that was taking place in my life with 'that woman' in it. The move to the new house away from my Grandparents was tough and now I was spending much of my time in the dark basement in the new house. I was not in control of anything in my life and I was starting to suffer. I was always emotional and never had any control over those emotions.

One evening shortly after moving into this house, Dad told me that he was going to meet with Mom and my Stepdad at a local restaurant. I had no idea why that was but I was to watch my brother while they went out. When they came home, Dad came down and said that my brother was leaving to go and live with Mom. Only one of us could go and he was the one. I never understood at the time what happened or why this was the case, but I was happy that he was getting out. He was much younger than I was and at least he could escape. I helped him gather his few belongings and said goodbye. We were never really close and never would be either. I was glad that he got out but also jealous that he got to go and live with our Mom and away from 'that woman'. I wanted to get out also. I wanted out of the basement. No one was coming for me however. No one. I was on my own.

It didn't take long for me to start breaking down and crying at the new school. I always knew when it would happen because I could feel the anxiety start to peak or build up. My tears would start to flow, my breathing would change and my shoulders would shake. The tears would flow so fast that my face would be covered in water right away. The nose would start to run and I was simply a mess. This started in grade three and continued for years to come. As hard as I tried to hide my emotions, some kids at school would see me struggle and they would laugh.

Shortly after, the tears followed, I was called names like 'suck' and 'cry baby'. The names hurt of course but I think they really upset me because I had so much pressure at home as well. I couldn't stop the tears, I couldn't speak even if I tried. I could only cry. I think this was one of the reasons why no one would really come near me in those early years to be my friend.

Now that I was a target for the bad names, it would become a daily occurrence. I would simply cry and then do what I could to cover my face or get away from them. This never happened in front of adults of course since bullying is so secretive. The last thing I wanted was an adult to see this anyhow. It was humiliating and I always hoped it would just fix itself in time. I always hoped that tomorrow would be so much better. I was holding so much in from the abuse going on at home and on weekends when we went to that family's house. I never felt like I had a way to vent or release some of the stress.

Although school was the time that I could be out of the basement, the truth was that going to school was no better than the basement. It was just different.

By the time I was in grade six , I was really beginning to struggle. The basement was the same and so was the yelling I experienced daily at home but school was getting worse. The name calling and my breaking down in tears was increasing. It wasn't just name calling anymore, now people were pushing me in the hallways, knocking books out of my hand and tripping me from behind. One of the most routine things that was done to me was to have my chair pulled out from under me just as I was about to sit down. I would then fall back on the floor right on my tailbone. The laughter spread throughout the class and I knew that I was the target.

We never called this sort of behaviour 'bullying' back then. I don't remember what it was called but certainly not that. There was no talk about this at school and certainly nothing reported in the media. To me, it was just a part of my day.

With my low self-esteem I reasoned that if no one liked me at home, why would anyone like me at school. That isolation was a feeling that I would become accustomed to. When I would finally put my head on the pillow at 9pm each day, I would be exhausted. I would also be hopeful that when I opened my eyes again, things would be better.

My routine was set. I would wake up and my clothes would be set out for me on the floor just inside my bedroom door. 'That woman' would pick my clothes out the night before and put them on the floor. With very little space available in the room, the floor was the only place to put them. I would wake up to my alarm clock and put my clothes on. I never had any choice in this. I would certainly never change what she had put out. That would have been really bad. I would take a deep breath and open my bedroom door. I would freshen up in the washroom and then slowly walk downstairs. I always knew she would be down there making her coffee and wearing her nightie.

As soon as I got to the kitchen it was the same old routine. She would scowl at me, and turn her back as I went about making my breakfast of cereal with milk and a glass of juice. I would sit at the table and eat it quietly and as quickly as I could. No matter how quiet or quick I was, she always made the time to say something cruel. If it wasn't about the way I dressed, it would be about my hair or how loud I was eating my cereal. Other times it was to simply yell at me about how she expected me to get home immediately after school to be in that basement. I'm not sure what she expected me to be doing otherwise but I always just responded politely. More often than not, just being in her presence would have me in tears and that was always the start of something bad. If she saw any tears, she would tear a strip off me.

She too would laugh at me when I cried. She would start by asking something like, 'What the hell is wrong with you?' or 'Quit your bloody crying!'. Of course I simply couldn't stop.

I wasn't in control. She never offered to talk about it or ask why I was crying, because she wasn't interested in fixing the situation. She was never going to be someone I could trust anyhow. I would do what I could wiping my face on my sleeve and just try to finish the breakfast so I could get away from her. I wished she would just leave me alone.

On the way out the door, she would shout things like 'You had better get better marks today' or 'Don't cry in front of everyone, you suck'. That was the way our morning would end together. Then, again right on queue, my anxiety would begin to spike on the walk to school because I always knew what was going to take place for the next several hours. By the time I got to the school itself, after about a 20 minute walk, I would already be near tears, if not crying.

Once I got to school, I would always go directly to my locker and hide as best I could. I never made eye contact with anyone, I never hoped to see anyone. I just wanted to be invisible and to have the strength to get through yet another day. As soon as I got into my seat in my first class, the name calling would start. And so it went: the cycle of tears, then others laughing at me and the dread of counting down the minutes until I could leave. I would watch the other kids and see how they were all laughing, smiling and enjoying treats. I was always wondering why they had candy and sweets but I never did. I wasn't able to process how I was being treated so differently from the others. I wasn't seeing how I was being neglected at home yet. I just thought that I was being treated the same as everyone else…until I came to school and saw the differences.

Without ever being given any money for treats and with wanting to be like everyone else, I decided to steal a chocolate bar one day before school started. I went into the corner store across from the school and took one. I didn't have any money and I knew that what I was doing was wrong. My heart was pounding but I just wanted to be normal. I walked out the door and crossed the street to the school. I didn't see the store owner come up behind me and grab my arm. He had called the Principal in advance and the Principal met us in the parking lot. The Principal took me to his office and called the Police.

A Police Officer came and put me in the back of his car and drove me to my house. I was an absolute mess with fear, tears and crying but there was no stopping what was about to happen. The Officer took me to the front door, the door I was never allowed to go through, and knocked. 'That woman' answered the door with a smile and a look of disappointment when she heard what I had done. She thanked the Officer for bringing me home and told him that she would take care of it.

Once that front door closed, she grabbed my arm good and tight and dragged me to the basement door. She was screaming the entire time at me as I cried out in pain and fear. I had no idea what was about to happen but I knew it would be extreme. She opened the door to the basement and tossed me down the steps. I was able to get my balance quickly but had to keep going down the steps as I didn't know if she was behind me or not. I ran down the rest of the steps, jumping down the final few so no one could grab my ankles from underneath and ran over to my couch. Tears were falling like bread crumbs on the ground and I was hyperventilating.

She never did follow me but she stayed at the top of the stairs just screaming while banging a wooden spoon against the door frame. She would often use the wooden spoon as a tool to threaten me. She would say things like 'you had better hope I don't come down there with this'. All the while, screaming every bad name you can imagine. I just curled up in a ball on the couch and cried and cried. I knew that she would tell my Dad and he too would be upset with me. Top it all off, the very people that I dreamed of being, the Police, were also upset with me.

My world was crashing.

Dad came home shortly after and she screamed at him for a few minutes. I was then yelled at to come upstairs immediately. I went up and she was furious. The anger and rage was clear on her face. Dad was standing there with a belt in his hand. She told him to hit me with it and teach me a lesson. I could see his hesitation but I also knew he had no choice. He sat down and pulled me over his knee and so the horror began. In a way it was similar to the feelings of when I was being sexually abused and wanting to be outside of my own body. I wanted to be somewhere else; to find a place in my own mind to hide. This was the first time that Dad was abusing me and clearly it would be a memory that would never leave my mind. I was hit by his belt over and over.

She stood there and just watched, telling him to hit me harder to teach me a lesson. She complained how embarrassed she was that the Police were at her house, and to make sure that I never did this again. I was an embarrassment to her and the family. When they both had enough, I pulled my pants back up and ran downstairs. That spanking was life changing as things would be much different now. The only person that I somewhat trusted had now hurt me and I felt like I had lost my only friend.

By the time grade six was about to end, I knew that I was going to be changing schools for grades seven and eight. The new school was much closer to our house and maybe only a ten minute walk. Although some might have been excited to change schools and have a fresh start, I wasn't feeling so good about it because the same students who were with me in grade six were going to be going to the new school as well. Even during the summer, when most others were so excited to have the time off school, was not a fun time for me. It just meant I was alone in the basement taking one day at a time.

Grade seven was worse than grade six for me. The bullying was intensifying from name calling and pushing to becoming closer to assault. I was tripped in the halls, pushed down the stairs and called names daily. Although there were many new students in this school, no one was coming up to me to be kind or even to say 'Hi'. I knew that no one was going to come around me because they would be afraid that if they were seen with me, they could be that next target. They just stayed quiet and stood there while the abuse was taking place. They never did say anything or even laugh when the others did, they just stood there quietly. I now know that with them standing there, it made it all much worse because they were acting as the bystander, one of the two things a bully needs in order to be effective. The bully needs the audience and he or she needs the target to relentlessly taunt. That was easy for them; they had me. They had already used me as a target for years but things would continue to get worse.

I was afraid to go to the washroom because they were not safe places. I understood that I would be alone in there and if a bully happened to walk in, I would be trapped. I did everything possible to stay out of washrooms and just stay in public places. I would try to find adults and stick close to them but they had a lot to focus on and I was always too shy to try to strike up a conversation. I ate my lunches in the corner, or somewhere away from others, but still in the public eye. There weren't many options at this school for me. I didn't have any classes that I excelled in nor did I have any favourite teachers.

I always felt like I was the only one who felt this way. I never thought that anyone else could be getting bullied or being abused and neglected at home like I was. I truly believed that it was just me and that no one would ever understand. Even if I did have the courage to reach out and talk to an adult, I could only think that their reaction would be to speak to the bullies and tell them what I had said. I knew that that would only make it worse. I wouldn't dare speak about the house and its basement because I knew that would be the worst decision possible. If anyone ever spoke to Dad or 'that woman' I would have been in so much more trouble.

I would spend my time watching the other kids and wishing that I could be like them, because I had never had a group of friends, or played, or never did anything fun at school. I just couldn't imagine what it would be like. I would sit off to the side, aware of my surroundings and just watch. I could see who the popular ones were, who the 'cling ons' (that's what I used to call the ones who were just there and not really adding anything to the group) were and who the less popular were. It was fun to watch and learn.

By the time grade eight started, the assaults at school were the worst yet. I was being sucker punched in the hallway, pushed all of the time, kicked and spit on while walking to class. When I was in class the name calling would be relentless. It was like everyone enjoyed seeing me cry and the fear in my eyes. As painful was it was for me, I just kept holding it all in. I guess I just hoped that things would fix themselves. I never contemplated telling anyone or asking for help. That was out of the question for me because I was convinced that I was the only one who felt this way. I also believed that the adults would only make it worse.

Dad and 'that woman' were now going to have a child together. This didn't change anything for me while she was pregnant because my routine was always to be in the basement or at school. Having another child wasn't going to change me or what I had to do. I knew their new child wasn't going to be treated like I was however. They had a daughter and she was the love of their life. She would never be allowed in the basement and could do everything that I couldn't. She could play outside, have friends over, watch TV in the living room, eat dinner at the table each night and sleep in a large bedroom all to herself. Because of this, we would never really get to know each other. With the large age difference, we would never be close and rarely speak. She was given gifts all of the time and certainly was the light in their eye. She was also never screamed at!

High school was the next step for me. This started in grade nine. The good news was that I would meet an incredible teacher named Mr. Ross. He was by far my favourite teacher and he would be like a mentor to me through the years. Mr. Ross would never know just how much he meant to me but he truly did mean the world. He would be my law and computer teacher all through high school. He was my pillar of emotional support as the years would go on.

All the while the bullying continued, since the same boys had followed me through the school system and tormenting me was a part of their daily routine. The crowds would get larger as they watched it all take place. I was still doing all that I could to hide what was happening and did what I could to smile or at least keep a straight face, especially in front of teachers as I never wanted them to see my pain.

One day after school, I followed the same routine as

always.

I heard the bell go which meant the day was over and, as always, my anxiety spiked. I instinctively knew that it was time to go home. I started my walk home that wintry day and could tell that I was being followed by two of the usual boys. They had consistently tormented me every day at school for years. I would constantly look back at them and saw that they were there but not gaining any ground on me. They were calling me names and I was crying but they weren't coming closer. I'm sure they could have seen the tears on the sidewalk as they followed me.

Once we got closer to my house, I ran as hard as I could and ran inside. No one was at home yet so I was alone, but I could hear the front door being tugged on. It sort of sounded like a cat scratching at the door. When the sounds stopped, I went upstairs to check and saw the front door was covered in spit. I was petrified and humiliated all at once. The first part being that if 'that woman' came home anytime soon, she would see me upstairs AND also blame me for the disgusting sight on the door. I was humiliated because I had to clean this up and fast. It was cold outside and the spit had frozen to the door. I had to use my fingernail to scrape it all off. The lowest of the low is how I was feeling at that moment.

On top of struggling with the daily torture of being bullied at school and the abuse at home, I was now struggling with something else that I couldn't figure out. In high school, everyone seemed to be dating the opposite sex. They would hold hands or put their arms around each other. I saw this more and more often through the years. I never really understood it because I didn't want to do that. With my mind always wanting to watch others and learn, I couldn't figure out why this was happening. I was looking fondly at the same gender. I was looking at the guys in school and wanting to be their friends so badly. I wasn't looking at them like a 'normal' person might; I was looking at them like I wanted more.

My body was going through puberty. I knew this because the hair on my legs was slowly growing in from my ankles to my thighs, slowly creeping in higher up my legs. My voice was changing and so was my mind when it came to relationships. I never saw any other guys watching guys. I didn't understand why I was. Of course I know now that I was gay but at the time I had no idea. We never had any gay characters on TV, no gay-straight alliances in school nor any books. I had never even heard of the word. Here I was thinking yet again that I am the only person that feels this way. My world was crashing. Far too much to hold onto and struggle with on my own. I still had no one ask why I was different from other boys my age.

By the time I was sixteen years old, that's when I knew that I was struggling with mental illness and was also depressed. Every aspect of my life that I looked at held nothing but darkness. I saw no way out of it. I could have random conversations with Mr. Ross but they were awkward because I never knew what to say and never really had the time. I could never stay after school as I had to get home right away but I also wanted to be in his presence as much as I could.

Sometimes, when 'that woman' and Dad were drinking with the neighbours upstairs, they would allow the guest's kids to come downstairs and play with me. Although that rarely happened, 'that woman' would often find a way to destroy those rare opportunities for me to have a friend. Although that rarely happened, 'that woman' also found ways to destroy that. She would come down to the beer fridge and make humiliating comments like how I was jerking off in the bathtub or how I had body odour. Little things like that just tore me apart. Of course the other kid would laugh and I just wanted to be alone.

Dad's drinking was now a daily part of his life. Sometimes he would get so drunk that in the middle of the night when he would go to the washroom, he would confuse my bedroom for the bathroom. He would pee in the corner of my room, right where my clothes would be set out for the next day. I would wear them the next day no matter what. I wouldn't dare change what had been set out or even tell my Dad what happened. There was no way out.

There was one Saturday afternoon while I was in the basement when I heard a knock on the front door upstairs. I could tell by the floorboards creaking that 'that woman' and Dad were going to the door. As it opened, I heard voices that I didn't recognize and some laughter which is not a sound one would hear in my house very often growing up. I could tell that we had some company that had come over and they were going to stay for awhile. The floorboards creaked until they all were seated in the living room and they started to talk.

I could hear everything downstairs and knew they were having a good time. Although we rarely had company come over, I knew that this was good news for me. I always knew that for as long as the company was there, I would be safe. She wouldn't call me names, she wouldn't scream and she wouldn't even come downstairs. I knew that I was safe and always wished the company would just stay forever. While they were up there having a great time, I was in the basement nice and calm. I was at peace for a change knowing I would be left alone.

All of the sudden, she screamed out, 'Tad, get up here!' my little heart began to pound and my anxiety spiked.

I walked upstairs slowly but convinced myself that I would be just fine because there was company over. The door was unlocked so I went into the living room and stood there.

I was only in the room for fifteen seconds but I remember everything about that time. I remember where everyone sat, their clothing, the smells, the way the sun was shining through the windows onto the carpet and, of course, I can tell you what happened. As I stood there, without saying a word, she was sitting directly in front of me on the couch with my Dad to her right. On the other couch sat two adults that I had not met before. She was also pointing at me.

She said, 'This, this is Tad. This is the half that no one would want'. That's exactly what she said to me in order to introduce me to the company. She was clearly comparing me to their daughter as being the other half. I never said anything. I just looked next to her to see what my Dad was going to say or do. Sadly, there was no reaction at all. He didn't even look like he was in the room. Expressionless. I looked back to her and she started to smile and snicker. I then looked at the two adults and they also started to laugh.

I remember just thinking to myself that nothing really surprises me anymore and I walked downstairs. I never did say a word. The door slammed closed behind me and I broke down in tears as I walked down the stairs. These tears however were much different from all of those years worth of crying before. I learned so much about my future in those fifteen seconds.

That was the first time that she had ever been cruel to me in front of other people. Until that day, it was a dirty little secret behind the four walls of our house. Now she was telling everyone exactly what she thought. I knew that my hopes of having her simply like me one day was never going to happen. I knew that if she doesn't like me after living with me for eleven years, that she wouldn't like me in the future either. There was nothing more that I could do to impress her, that was all that I ever wanted from her. I just wanted her to like me one day. I knew that waiting for tomorrow to get better was not going to work. Tomorrow was only going to be worse when it came to my home life.

The other part that I learned was that the two adults who sat there were not going to be helping me anytime soon. As a young person, all I ever hoped for was that an adult would one day see that I was locked in the basement and help me escape. When I went upstairs that day, those adults represented my dream of being saved. They knew that I was locked in the basement. They also had the 'bonus feature' of hearing just how cruel she was to me. My dream however simply vanished. No one was going to be helping to save me. My dream was crushed.

My tears were so different because I knew at that moment that depression wasn't the lowest that you can go because I was now suicidal. I wanted life to come to an end.

I wanted everything to stop. I didn't want to die however, just wanted it all to end. I wanted her to stop yelling, laughing and I wanted her to simply leave me alone. All that I wanted at school was to be left alone, to be invisible. Pretty simple really.

Even in my darkest times, with my darkest thoughts, I wasn't going to tell anyone. In my mind, I was the only one who had ever felt this way!

I had to find a way to get through this. Since I wasn't strong enough to reach out and ask for the help that I needed, I had to find a way through it. I slowly learned how to simplify life. I found things around me that I somewhat enjoyed. Really small things like the sun shining. When the sun was shining that would help get me through a day. I loved the sunshine! If it was sunny when I went to school and if I had one of Mr. Ross' classes, I would look forward to that because I enjoyed his classes so much. I simply found a way through all of this. Of course my struggle with sexuality wasn't helping but I found a way to almost block that from my mind as best I could for the short term.

My suicidal thoughts and depressive state would last for years. The darkness was there every moment of every day. My goal each day was to make it to 9pm That was my ideal finish line. As it turned out, my darkness during my school years would last until I was seventeen. When I was seventeen years old, one day changed my life forever and, in this case, a shift to the positive.

Running Away

Thursday night, seventeen years old and I just got home from school. As soon as I got to the basement, I heard the dreaded floorboard start to creak. I knew what was about to happen. I could hear the steps getting closer to the door at the top of the stairs and the doorknob turning. Like clockwork, she stood at the top of the stairs and just started to scream.

Every 'F-bomb' and terrible names you can imagine she was screaming at me. I hadn't said or done anything. I had come home on time, not said a word, and went directly to the basement. Just like I was supposed to. This however was routine.

I stood at the bottom of the stairs, just out of view from her and cried so hard. That too was normal. Even if I wanted to respond, I couldn't. I was crying too hard. It felt like only a few minutes later I could see the shadow of the family car go past the boarded up window in the driveway and knew that my Dad had just come home from work. Of course I knew that my Dad would never do anything to stop the screaming, but I was hoping that when he came in, right where she was standing, that maybe he could deflect it and give me the quiet 'Tad-time' that I enjoyed so much.

As he came in the side door, he simply closed the door behind himself and walked up the five steps to the main level to the house. He walked right past her without any acknowledgement at all. I could tell by the sounds in the house that he had gone to the liquor cabinet and got his rum and then to the fridge for the Diet Coke. She was still screaming. I could hear his footsteps upstairs going towards the door at the top of the steps and then the steps creak one by one as he was coming down to see me. Now here I was, face feeling like it was going to fall off because I was crying so hard and she is screaming so loudly at the top of the steps that the neighbours would have heard her. Dad on the other hand, was so calm and relaxed. He had his drink in his hand and came to where I was standing.

He stood in front of me with his rum and Diet Coke in his left hand and used a finger of the right hand used to mix it up and he smiled at me. He then said to me 'So buddy, whats going on?' in the calmest and most relaxed of voices. He was oblivious to the screaming and my crying. It's like he had a magical way of blocking everything about her out. Because I could never speak when I was crying, it took a bit to gather enough breath for me to respond by saying, 'Dad, she's screaming at me again!'. He said the same thing as always as he gestured with his right hand, as to brush it off, while saying, 'Oh Tad, just ignore her. She'll stop. She'll stop.'

Well as we stood there in silence, she never did stop screaming. He let out a small exhale and reached into his back pocket and pulled his wallet out. He put his drink down on the dryer and pulled out a $10 bill. He handed it to me and said, 'Tad, go on out. Go out and play with your friends and come on back when everything is back to normal'.

I knew right on the spot that so much of what he had just said was so wrong. He was giving me money and asking me to leave which he had never done before. He was telling me to play with my friends, he knew I didn't have. Then he's telling me to go out for a few hours and return when all was back to 'normal'. He truly believed that what was going on in my house was perfectly normal. I was stunned. I paused as I reached for the money and slowly put my shoes on. He stood right beside me. I have no idea what he was thinking that night or why he did what he did but it would change my life instantly.

I walked out the side door and saw she was at the top of the stairs still screaming. Something about me breaking up their marriage. I still have no idea where that came from but I guess I was her punching bag regarding their marriage. I walked out the door, looked back at my Dad and then closed the door behind me. I simply walked away. Eventually I stopped at a store and bought myself a Diet Coke and had a big gulp. It was almost like I was toasting my new journey that I had no idea I was about to embark on.

I had no where to go, no friends to play with and I never felt like I had any adults to turn to, so I just kept walking.

With only the $10 in my hand and the clothes on my back, I walked. I remember as the night got darker, I was thinking how I needed to go home as it was getting late. I knew that if I didn't turn around and go home now, I would be in DEEP trouble. As hard as it is to explain, my mind was saying how I needed to go home but my body was saying otherwise; it wasn't going to allow me to return. My body won, as it just kept walking.

I had never thought of this moment, never dreamed of it and certainly didn't plan for it. I just walked without knowing what was next. I had to admit that I am so glad that I did walk the streets all night because in the middle of the night, that is when reality finally hit me. After seventeen years reality would hit me so hard and within minutes. I realized that no one would ever be able to help me until I was ready and willing to get help. What I mean is that for twelve years of being in the basement, I was waiting for an adult to come and save me. The reality is that no one ever knew that I was locked in the basement because I never told anyone. Company would be told that I was downstairs playing. That is perfectly normal. No one would ever clue in, until now.

I was hoping people would help me, but yet no one, aside from those doing the bullying, ever knew because I never told anyone. I did everything I could to cover my face or wipe my tears. I didn't want anyone to see how vulnerable I was, especially adults. It would be a sign of weakness. I was doing all I could to protect my bullies in hindsight. I always felt like I was the only one who was dealing with bullying plus there was no attention being paid to this epidemic like there is now. There was no media attention on it and certainly not a spotlight on the subject like there is currently.

No one would ever know how I was depressed with suicidal thoughts because I never shared that with anyone either. I kept it in. It was only happening to me and I always hoped that tomorrow was going to be better. It got to the point that I couldn't wait anymore because waiting for tomorrow wasn't going to work because tomorrow was going to be a repeat of today and I used to HATE today!

In the middle of the night is when I realized it had to start with me. It was the next morning I started getting the help that I needed. I went to a Government office which helped with Student Welfare and walked up to the counter. I told them how I wanted to speak to someone and they brought me in to speak with a social worker. Now here was my chance to talk. Finally someone was asking how I was doing and I could speak freely. Granted, I was so frightened that I was going to be turned away and sent back home, but I had nothing to lose by trying. I managed to say just a little bit.

Whatever it was that I told her that morning, she agreed that I wasn't going to go home ever again. They helped me get an apartment and paid for my shelter and general expenses. I moved in right away but it was just a shell. It was essentially four walls with a yellow shag carpet. No food, appliances, bed or anything of the like. For me however, it was a palace. I knew that I had finally done it and escaped. I knew that she would never be able to find me.

My next immediate challenge was that I had a lot of work to do on myself. I had to work on the biggest challenge of all and that was to stop crying. For all of those years I truly thought that something was wrong with me but it turned out, I was perfectly normal. I was crying because I was terrified of her and petrified of being at home. Those years of abuse and neglect had taken a toll on me. As soon as I left, I knew she was out of my life, and not going to be a part of my future. In fact, no one would be in my life anymore because I was now on my own. No adults were going to check on me at night, to make sure homework was done or to make sure I went to bed at a reasonable hour. I could do anything that I wanted.

As that weekend came and went, I reached out to my Mom whom I had seen infrequently over the years and told her some of what was going on. I had been able to spend time with Mom here and there when it was convenient for 'that woman' to allow me to go out. It was always for such a short period of time when I did get to see her, always during the Saturday from 7pm to Sunday at 7pm time frame. As my Mom had married an amazing man by this time, my Stepdad, we would sometimes go up to his cottage located in Sauble Beach, Ontario. Although it took up 3 hours for driving each way, it was worth it. The cottage was such a beautiful place to get away to and the best escape from my reality that I could have asked for. It was quality time with my Mom and Stepdad while being on the water and being at peace. My Stepdad is such an incredible man!

My apartment was not far from her house and she was supportive right away; she and my Stepdad were always attentive. They were my pillars of support from that point moving forward. They helped me get furniture, appliances and food. I was building my life from scratch and they were always there for me. Although I was seventeen years old in age, I guess I might have been around twelve years old mentally and psychologically. I had a lot of work ahead to adjust to being outside of a basement. I had just spent the majority of the last twelve years in the dungeon.

As my first weekend came to a close, I was faced with what to do on Monday morning. Being on my own, I could have done absolutely anything I wanted. I am still proud of myself for making the choice to go to school. It was a very long walk now but I did it. First class that morning was Science and I took my seat on time. Like every other day, the boys who tormented me for all of those years sat behind me. It wouldn't take long before they started calling me the typical names. I heard them but nothing happened. Like absolutely nothing. I was part amazed and part confused. I didn't feel the urge to cry, no shoulders were shaking and my breathing stayed the same.

The boys would keep trying as the day went on and classes changed but still no reaction. That was the day I started to realize that these boys had no idea what I faced when I went home at night; they had no idea that I was struggling with mental health and they also had no idea that was the day they were going to lose their target because I wasn't going to give them what they wanted anymore. They wanted to see the sadness and fear in my eyes. It was over. I wasn't afraid. I had escaped the basement and this was my chance to start fresh. I had no idea that I was this strong deep down.

Those bullies simply moved on to the next person that wasn't brave or strong enough to reach out and get the help that they needed and the next person who would truly believe that they were the only ones to feel that way. They targeted that person and left me alone. I wasn't in the clear however, I still had my inner demons to deal with. Demons that would stay for many more years to come.

Tad eighteen years

Tad eighteen years

The Letter

Shortly after running away from home, I called my Dad from a payphone at school. When I told him that I wasn't coming home anymore and that I wanted to arrange to get my personal belongings back, he was very angry with me. He said that we could sort everything out if I were to just come home again. I explained that I wasn't going to do that. I was quite impressed with how firm I was with him and that I was not going to cave in. We agreed on a time for me to come pick up a few boxes and my clothes and that he would have it all on the front porch waiting for me. I asked if I could have the couch and table from the basement but he said NO and that I could do all of that on my own if I thought it would be so easy.

I was afraid to go back to the house but knew that I had to. I had some help from a few people who could help gather things up quickly and get out of there. I also called the Police to do a standby to ensure that all would remain calm. I simply had no idea what could happen and I never felt safe there. I wanted to be sure that all would go smooth and without incident. The Police did come but never had to get out of the car. Gathering my few items took only a few minutes in total and we were off to head to my new place. When I did unpack those boxes, I realized that I wasn't given any of my school work, photos or personal belongings aside from clothes. To this day, it's like I don't exist from under the age of seventeen aside from a few photos my Mom had.

As the days went on and I didn't have much to do, I had so many emotions going through my mind. One minute I felt bad that I had left my Dad alone, the other that I was so proud of myself for getting out. I was also very angry at times as well. I decided that my Dad deserved an explanation as to why I had left and to remind him how much I loved him. I remember writing the letter so clearly. I didn't have a table and chairs at the time so I sat on the shag carpet and used the dining room linoleum floor as my writing area.

I only had a purple pen and started to write. Turns out that I had a lot to say. I wrote many pages and decided to photo copy the letter to send them the copy while I kept the original. Below are some excerpts from the actual letter.

Mom & Dad

In response to your letter, I felt it necessary to speak from my heart and really tell you why I left. As you know, part of the reason was the rules and regulations, but there are several other reasons. Before I go into those, I want to once again say that the decision was mine. No one pulled my arm or encouraged me.

* * *

I realize how you have tried to make everything very tough for me on my decision to leave home such as you intervening in my receiving social assistance or not giving me any furniture but I would like you to know that there is nothing you can do to prevent my welfare

Please note that I probably won't need welfare as I have 4 jobs possible for the near future.

* * *

4 unrelated friends of yours have been in touch with me helping me out with anything and each have stated that there is a problem in that house and quite frankly dislike both of you for what has gone un-noticed in that home.

* * *

I was alone in the basement with no one to talk to or help me out when I had a problem so I was forced to keep it in.

* * *

So, being alone in the basement for 8 years, it's no wonder that my best friend are the Blue jays. Of course, when I did have friends over, ████ never hesitated to mention me supposedly jerking off in the bath tub as she indicated twice

* * *

There aren't enough excuses in the world to cover what you said and nothing you could ever say can heal my hurt. I don't understand how you could call this love?

* * *

I wasn't allowed to set it up for the past few years. The fact that there is no room is again bullshit because there was before. My liking to play baseball was constantly criticized because ▮▮▮▮ always said I wasn't any good. Yet, never once did she watch me play to say this. If I had a good test, there was always something else to cut up.

* * *

I want you to know, that what you have done to that home is just brutal. And this isn't not just me talking. Does mental abuse ring a bell. It can be just as harmful as phisical or sexual as I am just now finding out. Nothing was ever good enough for you. You have taken both of dad's son's away not to mention all of his friends. You ARE CONTROLLING HIM. You block out the fact that he is an alchohlic and can't see it himself. For 10 years I put up with what you call love. You can say that I am really mental but if you were to ask your "friends" they would tell you.

I have been told by 2 of your "friends" to change you and have a restraining order put against you both. This should be enough for you to see what you have done. You are dangerous. I can see that I have a problem and admit it. I think it's time that you did also.

* * *

And dad, please please get some help with your drinking. You are an alcoholic. It runs in the family. I wish that we could keep in touch but I know she wouldn't let us. So, maybe one day when you can break her chains like I am we'll meet up again and can start over. I just wish that you had listened to my pleas to you and did something about it. Can't you see, you have lost both of you sons. You are the only reason that is making my leaving so hard. You were my best friend and you will be in my heart forever. I love you so much that I can't tell you. I just wish that you could see what is happening to you. I miss you so much and having that father figure (and best friend.) It is basically impossible for you to find out where I am so maybe in a couple of years when this dies down, I'll get in touch with you. Until then, like I said, I love you so much, and maybe one day, we'll meet up again. ███ I think

you should look in the mirror and realize that it isn't the other people that are bad, it's you. Please leave my dad alone. I beg you. Keep the hell out of my life. You have done enough damage.

Goodbye!

Tad Milwin

After I sent a copy of my note, I began to receive letters from 'that woman'. Each one was taking responsibility and apologizing for what she did to me. She would say things like it was 'hard' to be a step-parent and that she just didn't know what to do with me. I assume the letters were therapeutic for her but I wanted nothing to do with them. I would simply destroy them after I had read them. She would send them to another address and that person would deliver them to me. I never did get anything from Dad at all. That was fine by me as I was still in a real dark place.

Although I had removed the stress of going home to that house and 'that woman', the truth is that other stresses in life replaced that. I was now living on my own, fighting to keep my grades up for the final year of high school while struggling to say Hi to people. I was also convinced that something was wrong with me because it was clear to me that I was attracted to men and not women. This was weighing me down. I didn't know how to cope. Like everything else in my life, I kept it sealed deep inside of me and never told anyone. I was careful not to stare or look at anyone. I was extra sensitive towards anything to do with sexuality.

Now that I was living on my own, word got out quickly and other students started to talk to me. I was the 'cool' kid at school now because I was the only one living alone and could have parties if I wanted to. I had a small group that would come over on weekends and we would party hard. Someone would bring the music and we would blast it as loud as possible.

Aside from playing games or have bottle cap wars, we didn't get up to much mischief. We were just loud and drank a lot. As much as I liked the company, I knew right from the start that they didn't like me for who I was, they liked me for my place. I sort of hoped that maybe they would get to know me and perhaps even like me. Since I had such low self-esteem, and was still very shy, no lasting friendships developed. They would make plans on other nights of the week like to go to a movie or Go Karting but I was never invited to those nights. That's how I knew that I wasn't a part of the group. I still allowed the parties on weekends because it was better than nothing for me.

I started talking a lot more to Mr. Ross after school now that I could stay later. I used to make him some cassette tapes with 80's music on it as I knew he liked that sort of music and he seemed to be very grateful for the gifts. It made me feel good to do nice things. He then returned the favour and got me two tickets to a Tom Cochrane concert which was at the former LuLu's bar in Kitchener, Ontario.

This was the world's longest bar at the time. Tom Cochrane was my favourite artist back then so I was really excited. It was also the first time I saw Mr. Ross outside of school. We had a lot of fun at the concert. I was even given a poster signed by Tom himself.

High school ended with me barely passing. I hadn't gone to school very much in the last year and a half but my grades managed to be high enough to pass. When school was almost over, I had gotten myself a part-time job at a general store in a strip mall across the street. This is how I slowly learned to be a bit less introverted and say HI to others.

Slowly I made more acquaintances and eventually friendships.

With high school now complete, I had a lot of personal pressure on myself. I had to figure out what I wanted to do and how I was going to achieve it. My Mom had been working at a very fine restaurant and was able to get me a dishwashing job there. I worked hard and made lots of friends. I proved myself and was rewarded with some promotions throughout the year. At the same time, I was struggling with alcohol consumption and doing what I could to avoid my mental health issues. I tried to keep myself busy so that I wouldn't think about my difficulties. My biggest issue was my sexuality and trying to keep it hidden. I was slowly coming to terms with sexuality as I still needed to make sure I was right about being attracted to men. I had to date a woman to at least just to have peace of mind. My time at the restaurant came to an end by the time I was twenty years old because I still wasn't feeling like I had a grip on life. I mean that I just didn't feel like I belonged anywhere. My new surroundings never felt like home. It was time to run away again. This time, I was going to run much farther away.

Rock Bottom

I stepped off the plane in Vancouver and took a deep breath. I only knew one person but wouldn't call him a friend. I got into a taxi and asked them to take me $25 dollars away from the airport. The taxi drove me to Burnaby and dropped me off at Brentwood Town Centre. I had never been to this area before, had no plan, and only a few hundred dollars in my pocket. I started to walk in the neighbourhood and found a house with a basement suite for rent.

I spoke to the family who said it might take a day or two for them to get the suite tidied up, but once they heard my situation, they made it their priority. We all worked together to tidy it up and I was all set.

The suite was a bachelor suite with a small kitchenette, fireplace and it came with cable. Although it was another basement for me, this was nothing like the past. I really liked the place and it felt like home. I could come and go as I wanted and there was the big mall right behind the house. My first thing was to go to the mall and I applied for a credit card. I was instantly approved and got myself a small TV. I was now all set. I had a place, water and electricity along with entertainment.

I went out and got a job at Boston Pizza and slowly met some new friends. One friend in particular really stood out to me. I think he was the first guy I really was attracted to, in more than a typical friendship. Of course, I could never share this with him. We did absolutely everything together. We would go on short trips to Whistler, long car rides or even take hikes in the mountains. We just hit it off so well. The thing was, however, that I liked him more than a friend and it started to show. I was always planning our time together and wanted to spend every waking minute with him. From his perspective, he had other friends and needed to see them also. I took that personally and it hurt. It was like he was pushing me away. I wouldn't dare tell him what I was truly thinking so I just kept biting my tongue. I think I was putting too much pressure on the friendship and me in general.

I was battling something that I had no understanding about and had no idea how to deal with it. I was torn.

Typically, we would spend every Saturday night together after work but one Saturday night, he said that he wasn't feeling well and we would have to find another time. My gut feeling was that he was lying to me. I don't know why, it was just how I felt. I was so upset but tried not to let him see it. At the end of our shift at work we went our own ways. I walked home as I lived just around the corner and he drove off. I didn't want to go home right away as I was just so emotional. It's tough to describe but I was sinking hard. I was caught between not understanding myself and also wanting to be with this guy. Friendship wasn't enough for me anymore.

I decided that I was going to go for a walk. The evening was dark with a light drizzle in the air but nothing that would make you feel wet. I just walked and walked. About eight blocks from my house, I came across his car parked on a side street that I knew was not the street he lived on. I froze right in my footsteps. My gut was right and I was feeling my heart pound. I was hoping that this was all just a misunderstanding but that wasn't the case. As I walked past, I heard his voice off in the darkness getting closer to where I was. He was holding hands with a girl and laughing away. He never did see me but

I sure saw him. Those tears that I hadn't experienced in a very long time were back with a vengeance. The walls of my world came sliding in nice and tight on me. I couldn't breathe. I was beyond hurt. I had been lied to and my past was coming back to haunt me.

I had never dealt with anything from my past, as I had been running since I was seventeen and now I had no idea about who I was as a person. I was alone and no one wanted to be with me. Even my friends, the ones that I learned to trust, were lying to me. I was done. I couldn't handle it anymore. I walked home slowly, crying hysterically the entire way. The rain picked up and was beginning to pour. I thought about my friend and how he was having such a great time, with a girl none the less, and here I was with a broken heart. Those thoughts only made it feel worse.

When I got through the door of my apartment, I was still crying uncontrollably. I went to the drawer by the sink and grabbed a bottle of Tylenol. I opened the bottle up slowly while I was in a trance. I was focused and only thinking about myself. I took a handful of pills and put them in my mouth as I cupped my hands under the taps at the sink and drank from them. I took another handful and did the same thing again.

With the bottle empty, I went to the bathroom and got some more pills that I had sitting around. Not sure what they were for but I was on a mission. My purpose was different now. I wanted to die. I was done with the pain and uncertainty. I simply could not do this anymore. I was done.

I walked into the living area that doubled as the bedroom and lay down in the bed. I never made any phone calls or wrote any notes. I never told a soul what I was doing. I went to sleep. It was over now. No one was going to miss me or even care. That's how I felt. Nothing would have changed my mind at that time.

It was the next afternoon that I woke up to a big gasp for air. My body was still and uncertain about what had happened. I was still in bed with no one around me. All was exactly where I left it. I was confused. I wanted to die yet I was still here. What happened? I tried to move but my stomach hurt too much so I just lay there. Eventually I sat up and was immediately very angry. I was so mad at myself for doing what I had, although no one knew what I had done, or tried to do. I was furious. I was an entirely different person now that I survived. I wanted to live and now I was afraid that I was still going to die because my stomach hurt so much.

I walked over to my Doctor's who was only a block away and told the receptionist that I had a bad stomach ache, however, I'm sure that was obvious. I went into the Doctor's office and he did what he needed as far as checking my vitals. All were just fine. I wanted to tell him what I had done but figured if everything came back alright, there was no benefit to telling him. I knew that I didn't need help anymore, I just needed to feel better. He gave me the all clear and I walked away. I now had a smile on my face; a smile that I would never let go of and would make it my mission to continue to wear. I never saw that 'friend' again. It was clear that my relationship with him wasn't healthy. Years later I would write him a letter. I knew that I couldn't work at that restaurant anymore so I quit.

Across the parking lot from the Boston Pizza where I worked at was Office Depot, and many of their staff came to our restaurant on a daily basis. I had met many of them so I decided to apply. I got a job and I met some of my best friends. One in particular, Lisa, is still the best friend I ever made. She and I hit it off right away. Lisa put me under her wing and we got along great. She introduced me to other staff as well and we would all party together at various places and venues. We were going to concerts, trips around the seawall in Vancouver and spending lots of time laughing and drinking. My drinking was not a problem by any means but it was almost daily now. It never affected work or anything like that but we sure did have fun.

One of the guys that Lisa introduced me to worked at Office Depot also. We got along so well that it was like we were married. In fact, many people commented on that as well, as we were inseparable. Not only did we do everything together but we also decided to get a place to live together along with one of our supervisors. The three of us would rent a house that was a bit of a wreck but we loved it. I got along great with both of the new roomies and we did a lot together. Not only did we all work together but we now lived together. We also had a pool table in the basement so we always had parties going on. I was a part of the cool group finally.

My newest friend and I would always stay up late talking.

His bedroom was in the basement and mine was on the main floor of the house. We were getting closer by the day and eventually go to the point that we would sleep in each other's bed. That was his doing to start with but something I encouraged moving forward. We would just chat and cuddle all night long. Although nothing ever took place sexually between us, I was ready to be close to someone. I was clearly in love and I thought that he would have known it also. Even our roommate would make comments and we would just laugh. One day he came to me and said that he wanted to travel to the United Kingdom as that was his lifelong dream. I remember he had said this in the past as well but I just brushed it off as just talk.

This time I could tell that he was more serious. I knew that I had a choice to make that would be really tough. Lose my friend or go with him. I had no interest personally in going, but I also didn't want to be without him. He said that he would pay for me to go and we would have the time of our lives. How could I say no?

Off we went. We used Edinburgh Scotland as our 'base' and would travel around from there. I got a job very quickly at a bar on the main street for the simple fact that I was Canadian and that was the start of something amazing. Again, we met so many new and incredible friends. We got a flat to rent and, to save money, just got one room with one bed. We continued our routine of cuddling in bed and talking. I was very comfortable but something still wasn't quite right. I felt like we needed to have a talk about our relationship just to ensure we were on the same page. I was also afraid to have that talk for fear that I would be disappointed. I just kept going with the flow until one night he met a girl. A part of me knew that this was going to happen but another part felt like he was cheating. It started to eat me alive again.

One night while he was out, I decided I was going to drink a few glasses of wine to get the courage to go out on my own. I wanted to go to a gay bar. After I had the drinks, I walked on over. It was a beautiful place that everyone knew about as it was very popular. I was so nervous but excited at the same time. It would keep my mind off my friend while also help answer some personal questions about myself. I waited in line until I finally got to the door staff. They looked at me and said, 'I'm sorry but this is a gay bar. No straight people allowed'. I told them I was gay (hardest words I have ever said) and that I wanted to go inside. They said, 'Prove it' while pointing at another doorman and telling me to kiss him. I was frozen. Never had I done such a thing let alone with a stranger who wasn't exactly good looking. Thank goodness I had some wine because I went up, kissed the guy on the lips and they let me in.

I went directly to the bar with my heart pounding out of my chest while being careful not to make eye contact with anyone. I was intrigued but also needed more alcohol. I ordered a bottle of beer and started to walk around a bit. The main part of the bar was on the other side of the dance floor that I was now starting to cross. As I did so, Stars on 54 came on with, 'If You Could Read My Mind'. I just so happened to love that song and stopped in my tracks. I looked around as everyone started to dance and that's when it hit me…I wasn't alone. In fact every single person in that bar was the same as me and they were all laughing and dancing. That song would change me because I would dance on my own and have the time of my life that night.

Although that night helped me with so much, I still hadn't dated a girl. I just needed to be sure. I met someone that I worked with at the bar. She and I hit it off quite well and I asked if she wanted to go for dinner one night. She accepted and we went for Asian cuisine. We ate and laughed all night long while enjoying a very large bottle of white wine. We walked to her house while stopping in a park on the way. We kissed a little bit but were laughing too much for it to be anything serious. We got to her house where she made it clear she wanted to have sex. She turned the lights down, put on George Michael's Greatest Hits (don't laugh, it wasn't my choice) and we started to have sex. I remember being on top of her and a horrid thought really hit me. I realized that I was doing something wrong and that I was going to hurt her emotionally. I faked the orgasm and started to cry. She would have thought that I was sweating but it was tears.

I went to the washroom and told her that I had to go. I felt terrible, not for myself this time, but for her. I put my clothes back on, kissed her goodnight and walked out the door. I knew that I had hurt her but I had the answer I had been seeking for twenty-five years. I was gay.

Coming Out

*N*ow that I had finally come to terms with myself, it was time to figure out what to do next. The amount of stress that had built up inside me over the years was about to start trickling away but I didn't know what the right way would be. I was also fearful that life was going to change for the negative. At this point all I had done was establish why I had been feeling 'different' for all of those years. Now that I had that sorted, I was afraid I was going to lose friends, family and my job. That might sound a bit dramatic, but it's the truth. I was so upset that my life was going to change in a negative way and I was going to be abandoned yet again after things had been working out so well of late.

My first step was sitting down my best friend and trying to tell him. I can't express how nervous I was. My heart was pounding and I was even sweating. I had a couple of glasses of wine to help calm my nerves. We sat down on the bed in our bedroom and I just looked at him and said that I was bisexual. Yup! That's right. That's what I had told him. I wasn't planning to say that but when I was finally ready to tell him, at the last second, I was too fearful to lose his friendship; I figured if I said that I was bisexual, it would be easier to reverse my words if things went wrong in our relationship than if I had I said that I was gay. His reaction was very simple. He didn't care, and he just shrugged it off with a smile. He gave me a huge hug and that was that.

The stress that I had been allowing to build up for all that time, that had almost taken my life, was evaporating slowly. I'm sure that my friend would have seen the weight come off my shoulders immediately. I felt terrific.

Nothing had changed. My worst fears never took place, and in fact it was the total opposite. For the next few days, everything was perfectly normal. I had an even greater appreciation for my best friend. Of course sexuality didn't come up in any conversation in the days following but there was no need to as nothing had really changed aside from me starting to open up. It was time to take the next big step. I again asked him to sit down a few nights later to tell him something more. I wasn't as nervous this time around but the words were still just as difficult to say. I simply told him that I was gay, however, this time the reaction was a bit different.

The reaction wasn't necessarily negative, it was just an awakening. He had the same physical reaction as before, but this time he also said, 'Nothing changes with us but just know that I like women'. It was like something inside of me crashed but was balanced with the release of yet more stress. The part that crashed inside me was the hope that he and I might have a chance to be together and take our relationship to the next level. The signs were there but it was unspoken. I had made some assumptions while also keeping my hopes up. He made it clear that, although our friendship would not change, that it also would not grow into romance. The good news was that I felt terrific finally saying the words, 'I am gay'. It took me twenty-five years to accept myself to get to this step. In my opinion, this was the biggest step I had made since leaving home.

Coming out is different for everyone. Some will come to terms with themselves much earlier in life, while others are able to declare at a much older age, if at all. So many variables come into play unique to that person. There are factors from family, to religion, to friendships to their own personal strength and meanings of comfort. Mine just happened to be twenty-five. I often wonder if I would have come to terms with myself sooner had there been role models on television or gay-straight alliances in school or perhaps information on sexuality taught in class. If there is one thing that I wish I could alter slightly from my past, it's that I wish I had come out sooner. Oh the stress that could have been avoided.

Now that the biggest step was out of the way, I felt I should tell my Mom and Stepdad. It was December and I was strong enough to take this step on the twenty-sixth for some reason. I still don't know why but I just had to do it. It had only been a few days since I had told my best friend and all was just fine. I was ready to tell my parents because, even if they did disown me, I had the support around me already. I had my best friend.

My Mom and Stepdad had never said anything derogatory or demeaning towards the gay and lesbian community but it was still a valid fear that I had. I was truly ready for them to walk away and not want to talk to me. Being on the other side of the continent at the time, I had distance in place to help buffer any negative reactions that might come from the call. I picked up the phone and dialled Mom's house. My best friend was sitting beside me and was an amazing support. Mom picked up and was as cheerful always. I said, 'Mom, I have to tell you something'.

She responded that she was just about to serve dinner and she would have to call me back. My heart sank as I knew the wait would have to continue, even if only for another hour or two. We agreed that she would call back when she was finished.

When the phone rang, it felt like days later. I answered but I'm sure she heard something different in my voice. I asked her to sit down but she had beat me to it. She just knew.

I took a deep breath and told her that I was gay. It was that short. I bet my voice fluttered with nerves but I got the words out. I felt my best friends' hand compress ever so slightly on my right shoulder when I said it. That was his way of showing support.

Mom said, 'I know'. I was offended. Of all of the reactions that I could have felt, mine was taking offence to her words. The reason being is that I worked so hard for all of those years to hide it, to make sure that no one would ever know and now Mom is telling me that she knew all along. She continued with the statement that she knew from the time I was just a little boy because she saw how intense my relationship was with the boys across the street from us when we last lived together. She said that over the years I would be telling her about friendships and such, but my relationships were always more intense when it came to males. Our phone call was short but it helped. I'm sure everyone could have heard the stress falling away from me like the air escaping from a balloon.

Mom would later tell me that when she hung up the phone and went to her bedroom, my Stepdad was lying in bed reading the newspaper. He asked her, 'What was so important that Tad had to tell you?' She updated him on the news that I was gay and he said, 'That's nice'. He put the newspaper down and went to sleep. My parents relationship with me would be stronger than ever.

You might have heard the saying that, 'When you come out of the closet, the door comes flying off of its hinges'. This could not be more true for me. It had only been a week or so since I had been to the gay club and yet life was speeding along, however, I had many more people in my life to tell.

I am asked quite often about the importance of coming out. Statements from heterosexual people, for example 'I don't tell everyone I am straight so why is there a need to tell everyone that you are gay?'. The fact of the matter is that heterosexuals do come out every day. Men can open up a magazine and be free to show a friend a photo of an attractive woman. They can talk about how their weekend was spent with their wife or girlfriend watching movies or the like. Women can speak about their boyfriends or husbands with ease. They can simply talk about their life without even thinking about it. Homosexuals cannot do this comfortably in public without first stating their sexuality.

I hadn't seen the girl that I had relations with since the night we had sex and I left. I was her supervisor at work and our paths crossed again on a Friday night in the pub. This was our very busy night and typically we had our highest staffing levels. We were all bartenders so we kept busy with no real time to converse, however we had smiled at each other when our eyes met. On Friday nights, our pub would have a DJ come in and play music all night long. Without thinking about it at one point, while the bar was packed, I asked the DJ for the microphone. I was the 'Canadian Bloke' and most regular patrons knew me. The music was turned down and everyone focused on me.

I looked at the audience of several hundred and said, 'I just want everyone to know that I am gay!' I have no idea where that came from but it's like my closet door flew right off the hinges at that moment. The room was silent until a single clap started at the back of the room. It slowly grew to the entire room clapping, hooting and wanting to shake my hand. I even got some chest bumps and kisses. It was done! I was out and certainly there was no turning back now.

What I hadn't thought of was the humiliation I caused to the girl I had been with. She was standing there and after I said what I did, she was mortified. I saw her run out of the bar clearly upset. I would only see her one more time moving forward as she quit her job immediately. I tried to ask to have a few moments to talk and try to explain things from my perspective. She wanted nothing to do with me. To this day, I am upset that I hurt her. I realize that I can't change it, and it was something that I felt the need to do. It just pains me that I had to hurt someone's feelings in that manner.

Nothing would really change in my day to day life aside from how I was feeling inside. My best friend and I were doing well and work was flourishing. Using Edinburgh, Scotland as my base, my best friend and I would travel for short periods of time to see other spots within Europe. We would go to France, Czech Republic, Ireland and England. As much fun as it all was, my love for him was still there and I couldn't stop it. It felt like we were dating to be honest. He however was still looking to date a female. He met one who lived in England and that started to cause some friction for us. I knew that he was straight but it was still painful to see the reality that we weren't going to be together.

Some weekends he would take the train from Scotland down to England to be with her. It would be a terrible feeling for me. As much as I was glad that he was happy, I was heartbroken. The stress between us was growing and we were starting to have some arguments which we had never had for years prior. I just didn't want to tell him that I was in love with him for fear that he would be creeped out and walk away. I needed him in my life. During one six week trip in Prague, Czech Republic, we had a fierce argument. It was different now. I could see that I was losing him a little more day by day. Perhaps he recognized my love for him and he was purposely trying to push me away a little at a time. Either way, we called the trip off three weeks into it and came back to Scotland. He also wanted his own room in our flat.

I had made several new friends in Scotland and wasn't as reliant on him by now. Of course I still loved him and hoped for the best but I didn't necessarily need him. He was spending more and more time in England while I was with my friends in Scotland. Every time he went down to England I felt a terrible pain inside but it would always feel so much better when he returned. Upon his last return, however, from a visit to England, he told me that he was moving down there to be with her. That was it. It was official that we were done. Within days he had packed up and moved away. We parted with a quick hug and I watched him walk off. After all we had been through, we called it quits. Believe it or not, it wasn't as bad for me as one might think. I was alright and I decided that I was going to stay in Scotland and continue building my life and my own identity.

I was so proud of myself for being authentic. I met new people, I lived my own life and I was flourishing. I would stay in Scotland for almost another year before deciding that I wanted to go and live in London, England for awhile. I had travelled there a few times and loved the city along with its vibe. I found a job in another nightclub and again, met many new friends. For six months I would party nightly and loved life, however, I still had a void in my life. I was lonely. It was time to return home to Vancouver and start focusing on the long term.

Tad, Tad's Mom, and Stepdad

Dreams Really Can Come True

Moving back to Vancouver came with its own challenges. Although I had removed a lot of stress and anxiety from my life, coming to terms with my sexuality, I was still struggling with certain aspects from my past.

Allowing people to get close to me, having self-confidence and making friends was difficult. I was cognizant of it all and wanted to overcome these challenges as soon as possible. Lisa and I were closer than ever and she helped me find a beautiful apartment right on the water in the West End of Vancouver. This area is well known for being a 'gay friendly' area including many gay friendly shops and establishments. The view from the apartment was incredible and I was excited for the future.

Lisa and I were always very open with each other and our time apart hadn't changed that. I was able to share how frustrated I was that I wasn't finding any success with dating. She and I spent a lot of time together having heartfelt discussions. We would walk around the seawall of English Bay, have a drink at a local pub or just watch movies. I decided that I needed to push myself beyond my comfort zone and take a chance. I had nothing to lose. I decided to look into some sports groups that I could join; groups specific to the gay and lesbian community. I always enjoyed volleyball and baseball so I decided to join a volleyball league to get started. The games were played downtown and very close to where I lived so it worked perfectly.

We all know how awkward it can be to walk into a room for the first time, full of people who know each other, but they don't know you and you don't know any of them.

It's intimidating and frightening and I had those feelings as well. I just thought it would be a great way to expand my social life. I met some wonderful people and made new friends that would help shape the person that I would become.

During this time, I had gotten a job at a University in downtown Vancouver. I was the Secretary for the Dean and worked Monday to Friday. The job itself was straightforward but there wouldn't be any opportunities for me to advance without taking some university courses. This was not something that I was prepared to do during that period of my life. After a few years, the job felt stagnant, no matter how wonderful my colleagues were, and I needed a change.

When I was twenty-eight, I decided to join another league for the summer. I joined a slow pitch baseball team. I didn't know anyone who played in this league but had heard a lot about it from friends I had met at volleyball. Everyone spoke highly about it so I signed up. I missed the draft when teams were chosen but was emailed by my new coach soon after and he told me that our team was having a meeting the following Sunday and it would be great if I could come out and introduce myself. I did and met two of the most amazing people, one of which was the coach and the other was his identical brother. They were identical alright, and it took me forever to be able to decipher who was who. We seemed to have a connection right away. I was like the third 'twin'. We all did absolutely everything together and were inseparable as time went on.

We played together a few years and it was when I was

thirty-two years old, at the start of a new baseball season, that our coach gathered the team together, as he always did, and something amazing would happen. A new player would join us that year and I would meet him. I remember going up to him and said, "Hi, I'm Tad and welcome to the team".

He shook my hand and said that his name was Shawn so I introduced him to the team. He and I sat down and started chatting and asked him early in our conversation what he did for work. He told me how he was a Police Officer. I listened as he told me about how he worked at the Vancouver Airport and how much he loved his job. I could feel the smile on my face growing from ear to ear as he spoke. When he finished, I told him how cool that was and how it was my dream as a little boy to grow up to be a Police Officer, and how I dreamed about it every day. He asked if I ever became a Police Officer myself. I smiled and told him that although it was my childhood dream, I was now too old but admired the fact that he was living his personal dream.

When he stopped laughing at me because I thought I was too old, he said something that would resonate with me and truly change my way of thinking. He said, 'Tad, one day you are going to grow old and sit back to reflect on your life. You will remember your dream that you wanted to be a Police Officer... and that's it! Why not at least try? You have nothing to lose but potentially everything to gain so that way when you grow old, sit back and reflect on your life and dream, that you can follow it up and say, 'and I tried". I was floored. Those words would resonate with me for the next few months to the point where I couldn't get it out of my head. Until that day, I had truly believed that I was too old and would never have put a moment of thought into it.

I was convinced that it was just a dream and that dreams are only meant to be dreamed.

It was at the age of thirty-two that I started to do something incredible and magical for me. I started to believe in myself. I decided to at least try because I had nothing to lose. I went to a Royal Canadian Mounted Police (RCMP) information session to learn more about the process and steps required to apply. The more I heard the more I realized that dreams really can be achieved but focus, hard work and belief in one's self is essential. I started the application process and worked closely with Shawn to learn more about the job. I wanted to know everything. He put me under his wing and brought me out on ride-alongs in Richmond. I would always stay the full shift of twelve hours because I wanted to truly have an understanding for the job. I wanted to see it all. Shawn was an incredible help. Each step for the application process would take time but with each step came either a successful completion notification where I would move onto the next step or I would be unsuccessful and unable to move forward. I was fortunate enough to keep moving forward.

The application included stages like a background check, medical tests, physicals, written exams, interviews, polygraphs and of course the physical abilities testing. I would always be sure to be well-prepared for each step by talking to current officers so I could learn as much as possible or research what was already on the Internet. Being an 'older' applicant, I had life experience which would be a benefit. I had no idea that having secretarial skills would also be a big asset. As the final steps were nearing, the nerves were really difficult to handle. To be that close to your dream and almost feel it was an incredible feeling. It was like having the winning numbers to the lottery read out as you follow along on your ticket seeing that with each number called, you have it.

On March 18, 2009 I got the phone call I never would have dreamed possible. I was successful in my application and was being sent to Regina for training with the RCMP. I was going to be joining Troop #6 which would commence on May 3, 2009. I would have less than two months to quit my job, give notice on my apartment, find a place to store my personal belongings and say goodbye to my friends for the short term. I would also have to do a lot of research about Depot in Regina as I wanted to be as educated as possible on what was about to come. No matter how many stories I had heard, videos I had watched or books I read, nothing could have prepared me for what was in store for the months at Depot.

RCMP

In April of 2009, I attended the swearing-in ceremony at the RCMP Headquarters in Vancouver, British Columbia (B.C.). I was there with five other successful candidates from all over the Lower Mainland. We were all nervous as none of us knew each other but we had that application experience in common. The connection was made between us right away, as we began the official start to the RCMP Training Program. We were allowed to invite two guests each and I chose to invite Shawn. He played such a pivotal role in where I was and he was so happy to be invited.

As the ceremony got underway, the six of us, who were Cadets, were asked to introduce ourselves and our guests. When it came to my turn, I was so nervous that I spoke about how important Shawn was but I called him Steve. Everyone broke up laughing when they realized the error and the ice was broken. We all felt much more comfortable and we knew that we needed each other as we would soon be flying off to Regina, Saskatchewan for the next six months followed by an uncertain future, regarding where we might be stationed afterwards.

On May 2nd, 2009, I flew to Regina and met with the five others from B.C. At the Regina airport, our 'Big Brother' troop met us and drove us to Depot. I had never been to Saskatchewan before let alone anything like what I would experience in the next few months. We asked so many questions on the drive. We were signed in and then shown to our barracks. We called it a trailer as it actually was a long trailer with thirty-two bedrooms which had curtains for doors that opened into the long hallway. There were washrooms at the far end and a small kitchenette halfway down the hall.

Everyone else was moving in around at the same time as people were coming and going. Luggage filled the hallways and strangers were introducing themselves to future friends. I was out of my element but, thanks to challenging myself in the volleyball and baseball leagues, I was able to hold it together and introduce myself to as many as I could. My room was the third from the end on the right side. It was maybe twelve feet long by eight feet wide. I had a small window which didn't look out on anything, a table to act as a desk and an open closet with two drawers. The bed was a single size with white sheets and a blue blanket.

As we all casually emptied our personal belongings into the storage space, we were cognizant of the expectations moving forward. We all knew that the expectations of us during training were going to be extremely high and there would be no room for error. If you did something wrong and were corrected, it was expected that the same error would not be made again. A couple of us that had met in B.C. decided to go for a quick dinner knowing that the next day was the start to our new reality. We knew that the next day was going to be the start to our new lives.

On the Monday morning, our first day of training, we were expected to meet in a classroom for introductions to some of the staff, our training personnel and the Senior Officers on base. It was overwhelming but one thing was being made very clear time and time again: we had better bond as a troop immediately as there would be no room for slacking off or messing around. The day was long as was the week. We spent much of it just learning about the history of the RCMP, expectations on base, learning where our training rooms and buildings would be, along with getting to know each other. We all had jobs to do as a troop and those tasks started immediately. First task was to keep our trailer spotless.

Every room had to be identical to the next. When we started getting our uniforms and equipment, it all had to be set up in a particular way and every item of clothing and sheets had to be ironed.

One of the things that stood out to me right away was the incredible eye for detail that was expected. To give an idea of what was expected, our beds had to be PERFECT. When I say this, I am not exaggerating at all. The sheets had to be tucked in perfectly with the hospital fold. The blanket on top had to be straight with no creases whatsoever. The top would be folded down the length of a clothes hanger and the pillow puffy and sitting gently on top at the head of the bed. Oh, and the sheets had to be ironed daily! Yup, that's right.

Every morning I had to iron my bedsheets. This would be inspected intermittently and if it wasn't perfect, the room would be tossed around and we would be back to scratch. Our entire team would be punished. I should also point out that our day started at 04:30 hours.

First thing each morning, our team leader would advise us all of what we were wearing for the day and we had to be ready to go, formed in a line as a troop, outside, by 05:00 hours.

Our uniforms had to be perfect. From the seams in our pants, which were perfectly pressed, to the collars on our shirts being spot on. We would be inspected each morning, no matter the temperature or weather conditions. It was not uncommon for us to stand there in snow, rain or the extreme heat of the sun. That's how it was. The hair on the back of our neck was inspected daily along with the length of our hair overall. If anything was out of line for any of us, we were punished by something called 'LA' or 'learning assistance'. This meant that the next morning we were to skip breakfast and meet in the gymnasium where a Drill Sergeant would be present to demand answers about why we had been sent there. This would be done publicly and with no shame attached. I ended up having to go to the gym a few times throughout training which, was never fun. The extra duty held up our troop as a whole, as we never left anyone behind. This exercise would set our day back by a few minutes meaning we would be yelled at for being late in our first session of the day.

Our uniform was earned as training went along.

Typically, to earn something like our duty pants (the ones with the famous yellow stripe) or our boots, we would have to answer questions posed to us by our Drill Sergeant about the history of the RCMP. If anyone got anything wrong then it was back to basics. Every troop wants to earn their clothing as quickly as possible to be the leaders on base.

Even when we did earn something, if we messed up, it could be taken away in the future. All the more reason to be as perfect as possible.

Training was very difficult; that's for sure. I don't say this lightly when I declare it was the most difficult thing I have ever had to do in life. It is designed that way. I was fortunate because I was there for one reason only, to get my badge.

As great as friends and partying and going to town might be, getting my badge was my priority. I was focused. I was working to achieve my dream and nothing was going to stop me. I went for haircuts every two days. I ironed my clothes daily. I studied every minute that I could. I ran between three and five miles every single day. I worked out, I asked questions and I studied hard.

Depot is a large base. There are houses and structures

for training. There are police vehicles, equipment, barns and open fields. There is a firearms range, a gym, a pool, the drill hall, a library, shops and the drivers training track. The track was the most fun for me. It's where we had to learn how to handle a car in many different situations, including control at high speeds, sharp turns, slippery conditions, and we were shown, as well as, experienced the capabilities of the car. Needless to say, we got to do things with those cars that I had never done before.

As we were thoroughly learning our skills, I wanted to start practicing them. I began to take my Friday and Saturday nights and do scenario-based training. Soon, several others in the troop wanted to do the same. While some wanted to leave the base and head to town to go to the clubs and such, I wanted to keep learning and homing in on my skills. I wanted to be the very best that I could. I know the others in the troop appreciated that as well. By the end of training, we would be told that our troop clearly showed how we had worked hard and practiced.

I always wanted to bring the troop closer together. I would often put together barbecues or sporting events at the field. I brought a Bose sound system to blast music from while we just unwound and spent quality time together. I would sometimes host meals by donation where the funds raised went to the Fallen Members Fund on behalf of the Troop. Depot can be very stressful and I wanted to do what I could to avoid that and keep us all as close as we could be. We were becoming a family as we had to rely on each other and, while on base anyhow, we were all that each other had.

Each week Mom would send the Troop a care package of baked goods. Something so small was something that the entire Troop always looked forward to.

When we finally earned our high brown boots, the ones

that you see when a Member is in the red serge, it took about fifty hours of hand polishing before we could wear them. When we received the boots the leather was dull and raw. There is no cheating when it comes to polishing the boots. Some people developed different techniques that they swore by, but overall, it came down to the same thing: we had to use good old elbow grease. It hurt! About fifty hours of doing small circles with the light brown, then dark brown, then clear polish just to get the base started was time-consuming. Once we wore the boots, if they would get dinged or scuffed or someone would step on them, we were back to basics. Next time you see one of those pairs of boots, take a close look at them and you can appreciate how much work went into polishing them.

While training was taking place, there were intervals when our external life would come into play. For instance on about week twelve of twenty-four, we were told as a troop what Provinces would be open to apply for a position. This meant that we were told which Provinces we could potentially apply for, and which ones were closed meaning we would not be able to go to.

This was not flexible. Ontario and Quebec were always closed as they don't have uniformed Members in those Provinces. Luckily for me, B.C. was open and available. We would put the top three Provinces that we would like to go to of those that were available.

On week sixteen we were told which Province we were going to and then asked to put together our top twelve cities within that Province where we wanted to work. My first choice was Surrey as I knew it was a busy detachment with lots of Members and opportunities for advancement should I wish to do that in the future. I then listed cities off that surrounded there and were close to Vancouver. It was on week twenty that we learned where we were going. There were many in the troop that were not happy with what they received. The truth is that we all knew what we were getting into and the possibility of being posted anywhere in the Country. This is why they recommend that you pack up all of your belongings prior to going to Depot so that you are ready to move as soon as you graduate. Even if two people in the troop wanted to switch with each other and do a trade, that was absolutely forbidden. Once the decision was made, it was final.

Of the thirty-two that started with our troop, we lost six for various reasons, from injury to unsuccessful tests results or just realizing that the job wasn't for them. We were really lucky as we all got along well for the most part and worked hard as a team. We had our drama of course which was to be expected when you see the same people day in and day out for months. At the end of it all, we were stronger and better individuals because of our experiences.

The last week of training was full of tests and challenges. This was where we had to pull everything together that we had been taught and apply it to scenarios and exams. It was very stressful to say the least, because if we were unsuccessful now, we would either be sent home without the badge or go back to basic training to start all over again. There aren't many second chances given. I was fortunate enough to pass everything with flying colours. I was also awarded the honour of having my name engraved on the wall at Depot for having run over 500 miles in the six months. Very few have ever accomplished this feat, but it was my way to unwind and have my quiet time each day. My troop was there, cheering with a ribbon, when I crossed the finish line at 500 miles. I was so humbled and happy.

Towards the end of training, I was told that I was voted

Valedictorian of my troop and would be required to give a speech before the troop, their families and friends, along with the distinguished guests.

We got our badges on October 19, 2009. My Mom, Stepdad and the 'Twins' were there to show their support and love. I couldn't have been more happy. When they called my name, I marched up, received my badge and just about broke down. After all of those years in the basement, all of the dreams that I never thought would come true, after the six months of training, here I was. I did it. I achieved my dream.

I gave my speech and have to say that I did better than I thought. I had never given a speech before let alone having been selected by my troop to do so. What an honour to say the least. I'll never forget that day.

Now that training was over, it was done. There was no time for celebrating as many in the troop would be flying out to their posts the very next morning. We had to go and pack up our rooms, get things ready to be shipped and get prepared for our new reality. We were Police Officers now and the next day would be the start of our new careers.

I had never lived in Surrey before, nor had I ever really even visited. With everything that I ever needed in Vancouver, there was no real reason to go to Surrey. It was now my home so I rented a condo, bought my first vehicle and went to the new office. Again, I had that feeling of not knowing anyone and being the stranger walking into a room. One of the first faces I saw was Adrian Oliver. He had this big smile on his face and was laughing when I first saw him. I think he knew that I was the new guy right away and he came over to say hello.

There was a lot to learn in a short period of time. I was expected to be out on the street working for real now in only one hour.

I met the team that Adrian and I would be a part of for a number of years. We had a team of about seven with a Corporal as our Supervisor. Our Corporal was a very experienced officer with over twenty-five years on the force.

He was direct and to the point. At first I found him to be intimating, but he became an amazing mentor in the years to come. I was paired up with a training partner for the first three months. He and I got along so well. He taught me the ropes and helped me to learn the city. Of course he also showed me exactly how things are in the real world. Until then, my only exposure to 'reality' was from doing scenarios at Depot. The real world includes many aspects that even Depot can't prepare a Cadet for. It took me awhile to see how not everyone likes the Police. Being someone who always admired them, it was a tough pill to swallow at first.

For the most part, once officers are done the training on the street, they typically drive on their own. I took to Policing quite quickly as a lot of it has to do with communication. I was fortunate enough that I had those skills. I was able to use my own personal experiences and techniques to help me along. Every day I was learning more and more. I still do.

Adrian and I would go to so many calls together along with another colleague. We had personalities that matched as far as being happy and positive. On days off we would try to get together when we could for dinner or drinks or just to relax. We were very close.

My life was perfect. I had put the past behind me, was living comfortably and I was now the person that I had always dreamed that I wanted to be. I achieved my dream and was happy. As great as that all was, things would change drastically one night in late October, 2011.

Jamie Hubley

In late October, 2011, I had just finished a twelve hour shift at work and got comfortable in bed. I started to read the news as I did every night and saw a headline that said something like, "Ottawa teenager takes his own life because of severe bullying." That was the night that I would start to read about an incredible young man named Jamie Hubley.

The article said that Jamie lived in Ottawa, and described the bullying that he experienced. It spoke about how he had a dream of being a figure skater and his family was very encouraging. They bought him figure skates, enrolled him in classes and Jamie went on to excel at the sport for years. He won awards and accolades, had a supportive family, and terrific extracurricular activities.

The article also spoke about how Jamie was bullied by a couple of students in school. In the early grades, the abuse was mostly verbal like name-calling. Jamie knew not to give the bullies the reaction they sought; he kept his head high, smiled and walked away. Bullies seek reaction.

There was also a report of Jamie being punched by one or two people and spoke about how the bystanders would not seek help, they did not participate, but they would just stand there doing nothing.

As the years went by, the bullying escalated and shifted to cyber-bullying on the Internet. Jamie continued to keep everything inside him. He dug deep within to look forward to the future. He looked forward to grade seven when he would change schools, and things would be different.

Jamie's first couple of weeks at the new school was fine, but then the verbal abuse started at school and on the bus. Over the winter, it grew into physical harm. It took some time but finally one of those bystanders had the courage to call Jamie's Father and tell him what was going on. Jamie's Dad came home from work, sat down with his boy and asked, "Little man, what's going on?" Jamie managed to say "You know, they've been pretty cruel to me over the years", and then told him about three boys forcing him to swallow batteries. Another time, he told his Mom that he swallowed the batteries on his own which would have been his first attempt at suicide. To this day, Jamie's parents do not know what really happened. All they knew was that their son needed help.

Jamie's Dad took him to the hospital for X-rays which showed Jamie had a stomach full of batteries. They said to let him try passing them for a week before they would operate. He did pass them naturally. The family got Jamie mental health assistance to help overcome the traumatic experiences he had endured. They also came up with plans, to help him move past all of these negative events.

Jamie's parents agreed that when Jamie was ready, he'd go back to grade seven in a different school where many of his friends from earlier grades attended. He would also always have a trusted adult with him going to and from school for as long as he wanted these things.

But at the new school, one particular person bullied him and it was severe! This time it was a girl. She told teachers he was doing things he wasn't to get him in trouble. She punched him and tried to get him removed from a school trip. Jamie's parents got involved and enlisted the help of other students to convince the principal that Jamie was the victim.

To get through these dark times, Jamie looked forward to the future, this time to a new school for grade nine. With high school now being an adult learning environment it was thought that grade nine would be much better. The bullying continued. In grade nine, Jamie quit figure skating, thinking that if he quit skating, which is what everyone kept making fun of him for, maybe they would stop. Jamie stopped but the bullies didn't.

His family saw that he wasn't going out as much after school. Instead, he was reverting to being by himself in his room at night, and writing on his blog. Of course there's nothing wrong with being on the computer—there's so much to do on-line and a lot of that is a teens social life. Jamie's parents weren't sure if something was wrong or if he was just being a teenager.

That summer, at the end of grade nine, Jamie opened up and told his family that he was gay. Jamie's family was open-minded, and there was a lot of growing together, communicating and understanding that needed to happen and that's what they did. They talked, all the time, about everything. Jamie started grade ten at the same school where he had been bullied all through grade nine. This time with determination, but not optimism.

He went straight to the principal's office and said, "I've been bullied for years, I've been in the hospital numerous times, and I want you to know. I don't want you to do anything because I've got a way to fix this."

Jamie explained to the principal, "The kids are not going to come up to me and be supportive in the hallway, locker rooms and classrooms because they're afraid if they are seen with me, they will be the next target. I propose that you allow me to have a classroom for one hour, that's all I need. I want to tell everyone in the school that, on that day and in that room and at that time, I'm going to be available in private and if kids want to be supportive or give me a chance and see that I am no different than anyone else, they can come and say 'Hi'. I'm going to sit in that classroom and I'm going to wait for them."

The principal agreed.

Jamie made up posters to reach the 2,000 students that attended his school. He called his idea, "The Rainbow Club," and he wrote the day, the time, and the classroom. He wrote, "Come and give me a chance, come and see for yourself that I'm no different than anyone else, just simply come and say 'Hi.'"

He put the posters up all over the halls. The bullying continued. Relentlessly. But now the kids were talking about the event he was putting on. Jamie kind of took that as a positive, and saw it as a light at the end of the tunnel. He wanted to make a safe, supportive place that was open for everyone to come. As the week went on, Jamie noticed his posters slowly disappeared.

That Friday, the posters were no longer on the walls – they were ripped up on the floor. When Jamie's Mom came to pick him up after school, she sensed that something wasn't right. Jamie said, "Mom, how's anyone supposed to know that I'm trying to do something positive if all of my posters are gone?" Jamie's Mom suggested that the family talk through the situation together when Jamie's father got home from work a few hours later.

When they got home, Jamie went to his bedroom and wrote an update on his blog. A short while later, Jamie's Mom received a phone call from one of Jamie's friends saying. "Jamie just wrote something on the Internet that you should be aware of and you should probably go check on him."

When she went into his room, she saw lots of empty pill bottles. She ran outside and yelled his name but she could not see him in the back field. She called the police, who said one of his friends had called them already. They were at her door in minutes. She called Jamie's Dad who came right home. A massive social media campaign with a full emergency services search and rescue operation began with 100 volunteers. So many people loved Jamie and came to look for him. Later that night, they learned that Jamie had committed suicide.

When I finished reading Jamie's story, I was absolutely paralyzed in my bed. I was completely frozen, an experience I've never had before. I read about tragedy every day and I also see it while at work, but nothing has ever moved me like Jamie' story. While being frozen in my bed, I could only think about one thing - being a five year old little boy and having a dream that I wanted to be a Police Officer because when I grew up, I wanted to be able to help people.

That was the night that I decided I was not going to be a person anymore who was going to sit back and read these stories and wait for the world to become a better place but that I was going to get out there and at least try. I was going to do something about it.

Jamie's story reminded me that kids were still feeling alone, still needing someone to talk to; still looking for friends and protection. I had to do something, but I had no idea what. I knew one thing for sure – I had to do something positive for youth.

A few days after reading Jamie's story, I watched my favourite show, the Rick Mercer Report, as I did every Tuesday night, where Rick rants about politics, and things that bug him. His rants are usually funny. I had not expected to see anything serious on the show let alone about Jamie, bullying and sexuality.

In that particular rant, Rick said that he knows firefighters, government officials, police officers and other people in positions of authority who are gay, but are not out. So how dare we tell young people that it's okay to be who they are if they're looking at us thinking but you're not okay with who you are and giving mixed messages.

Rick spoke about the importance of being who we are and being role models. Rick's message resonated personally with me as I was not out professionally. It wasn't that I was hiding it, it's just that it never came up.

I immediately started to tell people at work that I am gay.

I later learned that Rick is a friend with the Hubley family. It is a very small world and we are all tied together somehow. I decided that the next step was to connect with Jamie's parents, and sure enough, because Jamie's father works in politics, he had an email address online. It took me a while, but eventually I gathered enough courage and strength to put my thoughts into words, and I sent him an email.

I told Allan, Jamie's Dad, everything about me and how Jamie's story has really affected me. At the end of the email I asked if I could tell the world about his son. 'Can I tell anyone that will listen to me about Jamie?' He responded within the hour, quickly and briefly—he's a man of very few words—"Yes," and then, "Good luck."

The first word was permission to share Jamie's story and the second his well wishes. I am so glad that he said, 'Good luck' because I use those two words to this day to be my motivation to spread Jamie's message of acceptance and understanding in the hopes of making this world a better place.

Jamie

Tad and Rick Mercer at World Pride Parade in Toronto

Bullying Ends Here

Now that I had the Hubley family's permission to share Jamie's story, I had the drive to want to help and I knew that whatever I was going to create would be focused on youth, I had to come up with a name. It didn't take long to decided on the name, it was a matter of ensuring it was available on the Internet for a website address. I decided to call the program, 'Bullying Ends Here' as it spoke to the topic and the goal. My goal was to end bullying immediately. The domain name on the Internet was available so I grabbed that as well.

Things were moving along really well and I started to learn how to create a website. I had never done that before but it was fun. Just one page at a time. I wanted to keep it simple and not be filled with useless information. I worked hours per day for months until I was satisfied that it was ready to go. One of the most important elements that I wanted on the website was the ability to reach me directly. I put a 'Contact Tad' button on the homepage. The website went 'live' in early 2012.

Once the website was completed and ready, I then had to think of what else I wanted to do. I couldn't just stop there. It was just another website. I wanted to start learning about school now a days and see what its like to be in high school and compare it to when I was last there. I went to a local high school in Surrey, B.C. in hopes of just listening to a group that might be meeting on a lunch hour. I stopped in knowing that lunch was taking place and asked the secretary if any groups were meeting. There were two but the one was not available as they were outside. The second group meeting was the Gay-Straight Alliance (GSA) group. PERFECT!

I was taken to the classroom and my intent was to sit in the back and just listen. When I walked into the room, there were about eleven students and an adult facilitator present. They all turned to look at me as I was in uniform and they didn't know why I was there. I quickly introduced myself and just mentioned that I just wanted to hear personal experiences on what being a teenager is all about now and what it's like to be in school. The youth in the room just wanted to know all about me. The more I was asked questions the more I opened up and told them about the basement, my difficulties with mental illness and even about my sexuality. That's when a couple of questions came that really caught my attention. One was, 'How am I so lucky,' and the second 'How am I so fortunate'. I was floored. They really wanted to know how it was possible to be where I am today based on what I experienced in the past. I realized they were looking up to me. I thought to myself that if these students were looking up to me with my story, others might as well.

They weren't looking up at me for me per se, they were looking up to me as they were looking for role models in general.

That facilitator told another teacher in the district about me and I was then invited there. I was thinking that I might do this maybe once per month on a day off type of thing. I had no idea about what was going to happen.

What started out with sharing my story then turned into talking about Jamie as well. I then started to just flow with my timelines, as I have done in this book. As the presentations were piling up, and I was doing it all on my days off, I was also telling everyone about the website and the ability to contact me. I wanted to make it clear that people do care and they have someone to talk to at any time. Granted, I am not a Counsellor or anything like that, but I make a great friend who will not repeat anything they share with me and I'll always be there through their difficulties.

That GSA I spoke to took place in January of 2012. My first full presentation was to a school in Cambridge, Ontario, which was in February of 2012, and was the start of what would be quite the journey. I had received permission to wear the officers' uniform while doing the presentations from my Supervisor and was so proud to do so. I was especially proud to wear it in places like Ontario where the majority of youth never get to see a Mountie dressed in uniform; they were intrigued. The positive connection to students being made, because of the presentations, was priceless. I was now using vacation time to go to places like Ontario for the presentations. I never advertised the program or myself; I just went by requests. What would happen is that with each presentation, the adults would share with others in their network and then more requests would be made. I had no idea word would spread so quickly.

It wasn't long before the media picked up on the message and program. In March of 2012 I gave my first ever interview to a newspaper. I was nervous as can be as I had never done such a thing. I was sharing my own story but this entire program was new to me as well. I wasn't comfortable sharing 'everything' at that time as I am now. At the beginning I never spoke of my struggles with mental illness as I just felt like it was inappropriate to share my adult struggles. It wouldn't take long before my approach would change also.

With the presentations adding up, so were the emails. I started to receive dozens of emails speaking about self-harm and low self-esteem. I had to adapt quickly because, until then, I only had my own experiences. Some of what the emails were stating were things that I had not necessarily understood or even heard about. I read a lot of books, especially on self-harm, so that I was informed. I would always be there to talk to but was also cognizant of the importance of recommending the experts such as the Kids Help Phone and reaching out to trusted adults.

Requests were coming from all across the Country and I was paying for flights, accommodations and rental cars, all on my own. I thought that I should look into the possibility of receiving charitable status so that people could donate if they wished. I had to create a Board of Directors and do a lot of paperwork for this process. I did all of that and sent it off to the Government. I had no idea how long it would take but people were asking to help but they simply couldn't as I couldn't offer tax receipts.

By October of 2012, the media in B.C. were now picking up on my story and printing articles in the newspaper. It was getting the attention of the Senior Staff in Surrey who wanted to meet with me. I knew that the program was helping so many and that the positive connections being made for Policing were immeasurable. My supervisors were aware of what was going on as were my peers. I just kept work and the program very separate. Now my Senior Supervisors wanted to talk.

I went to the Deputy Chief's office and sat down. He had the newspapers in front of him with my photos and article there to see. He smiled at me and said, 'Tad, I had no idea that this is what you were doing on your days off'. Of course he didn't. I had never even chatted to this man before and I wasn't telling anyone what I was doing. I wasn't looking for recognition; I wanted to help others. He was thrilled and asked a bit about the program and why I created it. He asked if I would ever be interested in doing this full time and I said that I would be. He asked for it to be left with him and for me to keep up the good work.

I continued on with my policing the streets of Surrey and implementing the program on days off. The website was also growing to include a schedule and a place to add personal feedback. It was incredible what was truly happening as the emails were coming in by the hundreds per week and requests by the dozens. Word was getting out and the program was wildly popular. Work was going well as I was nominated for Police Officer of the Year in 2012 by my peers.

It was in December that the Deputy Chief asked me to come meet with him again. He said that he had spoken to the B.C. RCMP office and found a way for me to work with them on a secondment of three months to focus on the program. I had mixed feelings as I wanted to still be on the road doing my general policing duties as a first responder, but I was also amazed that my employer was so pleased with my work that they thought it worthy of doing it full time. I was to report to the B.C. RCMP Headquarters which happened to be located in Surrey. I was nervous along with being so excited. It was only for three months and my schedule for this period of time was already full so it basically allowed me to focus on the program. I was introduced to my new team and Inspector, and shown to where my desk would be when I was in the office. My Inspector asked for my presentation schedule to which I provided. It included trips throughout B.C. but also to Alberta, Manitoba and Ontario. She explained that the unit would not be able to pay for those trips. I was not looking for that anyhow as I had already planned this to be done on my vacation time and at my own expense.

About two weeks later, my Inspector returned to meet with me and said that there had been a reversal and the RCMP would in fact pay for my out-of-pocket expenses.

I was not expecting this and it took me off guard. I was so thankful. The program was to continue on exactly the way I had created it. The same story, the same website, the same reference cards as I had done prior to joining this unit. I knew however, that something wasn't feeling quite right. It's hard to explain but it was just a gut feeling I had.

I started to notice that when I was in the office, my Corporal would never speak to me. There were eight of us that worked in the office and it was an open space concept. He would make it a point to come and say, "Hi" to each and every person but would never acknowledge me. He just walked past. My peers would look at me and sigh as the man did this every morning but I didn't mind. I did speak to my Inspector and the Staff Sergeant about this but they both brushed it off saying that was just the way he was and that when he got to know me and the incredible work that I was doing, that he would come around. When this never changed and I addressed it again, I was then told that he was upset that I had come into the unit and money was being designated to cover the expenses when he had worked there for years and he struggled to get the funding in the first place. They were feeding me excuses instead of addressing the problem. This behaviour was accepted! I held my head up high and would always say, "Hi" no matter what.

The media exposure was growing at an incredible pace as people were hearing my story and how one person had created something that had exploded in such a short period of time. The results were being reported on and lives were being saved. The RCMP also put me in front of the cameras to share my story and even featured me in their own Quarterly Magazine speaking about the program. One day while I was at Costco, the Commissioner of the RCMP called me on my personal phone to congratulate me on my work and advised me that word had gotten all of the way back to him. He told me how proud he was and with how much courage he felt I was exhibiting.

In the first year alone, the program reached just shy of 20,000 students in schools in four Provinces. It was full steam ahead and a lot of heads were being turned.

I still had a gut feeling that something wasn't right as it just seemed too good to be true. Early in January, my Inspector sat me down and said that because of the overwhelming demand for the program, she was able to find the funding to continue having me seconded until the end of June, 2013. I felt on top of the world. She asked if she could come and see a presentation along with asking others in my office to see. Everyone came out to watch at some point.

In March is when my Inspector came to a presentation in Hope, B.C. She sat at the back of the room in plain clothes and watched. When the presentation was over and the youth had left, I asked her what she thought. She didn't answer the question, instead asking me to go for coffee. We met a local coffee shop and made some small talk. Inside me, I was nervous, as I really wanted to know what she thought since she would be the one making decisions on the program being extended down the road. She looked at me after about fifteen minutes of small talk and said, 'Tad, before you speak I want you to hear me out. I looked at your schedule and saw that next Thursday you are free. I have taken the liberty to make an appointment with the RCMP Psychologist where we can talk with him about what you are doing. How do you feel about this?'.

I have no idea what the look on my face would have said to her but I was furious even though I was not surprised. It was like my gut feeling was right all along. Something wasn't quite right. I simply looked at her and said that I would do whatever it took to show that what I am doing is working and helping others and has nothing to do with me. She had made this appointment without ever having seen the presentation and for whatever reason, felt it was necessary for me to speak to a Doctor. I went home that night and called my Mom, furious about what had happened. I had no words to explain what was going on or why this was taking place. The only explanation I had received about why this was done, was to protect me because I was staying in hotels by myself a lot. This person knew nothing about me and had not even taken the time to get to know me. She would have known I was staying in hotels for the last year and that I lived alone as well. I still have no idea what she was thinking.

I went to the appointment that Thursday and was met there by her. She walked into the office with me and introduced me to the Doctor and asked if it was alright if she left me alone. I felt like I was being treated like a child. She left and the Doctor sat back in his chair, looked at me and asked if I felt like I should be there. I laughed and said of course not. He smiled and asked why. I explained that if my program was making money and I was being paid for my efforts, I would be making a lot of money and people would pat me on the back saying how I deserved it for working so hard, but because I was doing this on my own and not being paid a dime, my Inspector felt that something was wrong with me. He smiled back and that was that. We spoke casually about life and some of his own background. He would later write an email to my boss, about which I was cc'd, saying that I was just fine and had passed with flying colours.

In March of 2013, my Inspector told me that she wanted us to go to Ottawa to meet Jamie's family. She felt as though this was important to help move forward and put a personal touch on things. She wanted to come as well. We flew in and met Allan and Wendy Hubley at Allan's office. We spoke casually about what I was doing and my Inspector was terrific. She helped break the ice and truly started to build a relationship with them. She went on to tell them that I would be in town a couple of additional days and how I would be available if they had any additional time to meet with me privately. They did and I would go to their home the next day. Allan, Wendy and I spent many hours speaking about Jamie and what his life was like. There were tears and smiles. I was embraced as one of their own and shown photos, videos and paintings. In fact, when I left, Allan gave me a painting that someone had made of Jamie. It hangs in my living room to this day.

In advance of the trip and knowing that we were going to Ottawa, I emailed the Commissioner to advise of our arrival and to see if he might have some time to stop in and say Hi. He emailed back right away saying something like, 'come hook or by crook,' we would meet.

I messaged my Inspector to tell her of this great news, fully expecting her to be happy for the time with him. It was the total opposite. She was furious with me, she said, 'How dare I email the Commissioner directly,' and that she was busy and would not be rescheduling her personal appointments to meet with him. She also told me that she didn't trust anyone in Ottawa. Needless to say, the meeting with him never happened.

March of that year is also when I received the notification that the program had received Charitable Status in Canada. I told my Inspector and Staff Sergeant right away as I felt that maybe this could help raise funds and expand the program. They were NOT happy at all.

They spoke of conflict of interest issues, the expectations of the public feeling like they would *have* to donate and how this was totally unacceptable behaviour. I explained that I did this many months ago and was only hearing now. I never did anything to solicit funds at all. I was told that I was not to mention this fact to anyone nor to accept any donations. Again, I was sinking in my feelings about how things were going overall. Although I was doing good work, I was feeling like I was in that unit to give them the credit and only because they had to work with me. I never felt welcomed whatsoever.

As the end of my secondment was coming to a close, there was clear friction between me and everyone else. The Corporal never did speak to me, my Inspector was absent a lot and I wasn't in the office for very long, if at all. My Inspector again sat me down and congratulated me on my terrific work to date. She spoke about how hard she had worked to secure funding for me to continue on with the program for another school year and that Surrey had agreed to the extended secondment. I was given a two page letter outlining the contract for the new position. It stated that I was not to hold any formal position or be associated with any external societies or charities and that I shall not endorse, sponsor or promote any external anti-bullying organization not approved by the B.C. RCMP. I would not be allowed to give out any business cards promoting the website, to have my own website closed down and that all emails received by me would go through the RCMP website and be monitored by others.

This defeated the entire purpose of the program as youth

weren't messaging me because they wanted to speak to a stranger or a random person, they wanted to speak with me. They wanted to go to my website to see photos and videos of Jamie that his family had provided on my visit with them. This was simply unacceptable to me so I politely declined and said that I would fulfill my current obligations until the end of June as originally agreed to, but that I would then want to return to my first responder role and I would go back to doing the program on my own time. I was told to leave immediately at the start of June and that Surrey was expecting me. No one even said goodbye.

This was going to be the start to the end of my service with the RCMP, I just didn't know it yet.

Adrian Oliver

As 'Bullying Ends Here' was being presented across the country on my days off, my peers at work only knew the basics of what I was doing. Of course the media helped them to understand that whatever it was that I was doing, it was big and effective. After inviting Adrian on numerous occasions to come and see the presentation for himself, he came with me in late October, 2012. He brought along his girlfriend whom I just adored.

I was speaking to a classroom of grades sevens and eights and Adrian and his girlfriend sat at the back of the class. I did my routine for an hour and then spent time afterwards with the students. Some were crying and others wanting to simply shake my hand. When they all left, Adrian's girlfriend came up to me with tears in her eyes and gave me a big hug. While she did this, she whispered in my ear, 'He loves you, you know'.

I took this to mean that Adrian loved me. One of the best things about Adrian and I was that we always spoke openly. We shared just how much we cared for one another.

Adrian was next to come up and he too gave me a big hug. He then pulled back and with his animated hands said, 'Buddy! I had no idea that this is what you were doing on your days off!' I smiled and said, 'I know'. I just never really could find the words to truly explain what it was that I was doing. It's one of those things that one just needs to see for himself. Adrian was so excited and had such a huge smile on his face. He asked when the next presentation was. Because I did them on days off and with his own schedule as well, we could only set a date that worked for both of us in the middle of November. That presentation was going to be for a large group in a theatre, so he said that he wanted two seats to come and see it again.

For the next few weeks, he and I spoke a lot by text messages. Of course we talked at work as well, but we kept ourselves busy and sometimes we didn't cross paths during a shift. He was so intrigued by what was going on with the program and the people that were messaging me. He would make remarks like, 'Are you going for lunch with the President today?' or, 'Let me know when Oprah calls'; little humorous things like that. He was just loving the whole scene.

On the night of November 12, 2012, I took the night off work. It was just a normal night that I figured a night of rest would help and there wasn't much going on at work. I knew that Adrian was going to take our last night shift off so, to help ensure our numbers were alright, I took the opposite one off.

I went to bed at a normal hour and slept soundly. At about 05:06 hours, my phone started to ring. This is extremely abnormal but when I looked at the call display, I saw it was a member of my team at work and knew they were just getting off work so I assumed it was someone's pocket dial. I ignored it and went back to sleep. No messages were left.

Shortly afterwards, my phone vibrated again; this time with a text message. It was another colleague that I worked with saying, 'Do you know that Adrian was killed in a car crash this morning?'. I had to look at this message a few times. I thought it was a very cruel prank. It took a few minutes for reality to set in. I ran to turn the TV on as the morning shows were now all on the air. Sure enough, there was the scene of the collision as the top story. They didn't have much to report on other than a Police Officer had been killed in the line of duty only an hour and a half earlier. My body went weak and I sank back into the couch. I just didn't know how to process this news.

I threw my clothes on and raced to the scene of the collision. I am the sort of person that just needs to see it for myself. The area was like a business park with a large area closed due to the accident. I parked my car and walked quickly but with very heavy legs. I could see in the distance what I had just seen on television. As I got closer, hoping this was all just a bad dream or misunderstanding, reality set in. It was clear from the scene that Adrian didn't make it and would have passed quickly. I just stood there, looking. The vehicle was severely crumpled on the front driver's side. The driver door had been removed by the firefighters who worked so hard to save him. A small cloud of steam was still hanging over the engine block which was now exposed. It was an overcast morning with a chill in the air. The area was very quiet aside from the voices of the emergency workers doing their investigation.

I slowly walked back to my car, lost in a swirl of emotions. I just couldn't process what I had seen. I couldn't connect the crushed car with the fact that Adrian was gone. Aside from my grandparents passing at an earlier time, death wasn't something that hit home for me. As I got back to my car, I sat in the drivers' seat before starting it up and stared out into space. I was waiting for the tears that would never come. I wanted to cry, I needed to cry but they wouldn't come. I was just blank. Perhaps it was the years of crying and feeling ashamed that keeps them away. Inside I was a mess but on the outside I kept it all together.

I drove off to our headquarters where all staff were expected to report. It was close to eight in the morning at this point and people's emotions were running very high as to be expected. Most had just worked an entire shift AND been at the scene. I can't imagine what they saw or what they experienced. I try not to think about it from their point of view. The RCMP was terrific, ensuring all staff were off work to grieve and just have time to process. Grief counsellors were brought in, meetings arranged and the local legion allowed us to use their space for days. We would all gather there and share stories. We would laugh and many would cry.

The day of Adrian's funeral also happened to be the day that he and his girlfriend were going to come to my presentation in the theatre. I know that Adrian would want me to be at the school. His funeral was set to begin around noon hour and I was an Honorary Pallbearer but I just knew that I had to do the presentation still. I remember that day so clearly. The school assumed that I was going to cancel knowing that a colleague had passed away and the funeral was that day. They didn't know how close Adrian and I were however, when I arrived, the Principal suggested that we postpone but I just had to proceed. The Principal was also the one that had reserved the two seats for Adrian but she had no idea that they were for him. When I told her that they were going to be for Adrian, she too broke down in tears.

She got up on stage at the start of the assembly to introduce me. Five hundred youth in this theatre and no one knew a thing about me. The Principal made it a point to tell everyone that two seats were empty at the front of the theatre because Adrian was supposed to be there. Everyone had heard by now about the fallen Officer and they were stunned. You could have heard a pin drop. I got up on stage and did what I always did. I did the presentation and let the audience know that if they ever needed a friend or someone to talk to, I was there for them. I gave them the website address and then departed for the funeral.

I raced off to get there on time and spent six hours with my friend one last time. We marched the route beside his hearse and then walked with his casket to the stage. The pallbearers all sat close to the stage and listened as his family, girlfriend and identical twin brother all shared stories and memories of Adrian. The arena was full of uniformed officers which was incredible to see. I know that my buddy would have been proud and honoured.

When I saw the hearse drive away with Adrian, I knew that would be the last time I would see him again. Adrian was gone, this I knew for sure.

I went home that night, exhausted. Not only physically but emotionally as well. I sat on the couch and opened up my laptop. When I logged into my email that night, I had to do a double-take. My inbox said that I had over 300 emails. When I started to read them, I saw that the youth from the morning presentation had taken my message to heart and reached out. Not to share their own stories but to show their support to me. One of the most inspirational days for me in this journey.

Adrian

Ultimatum

It was just after I had left the B.C. RCMP and went back to my regular policing duties that I did my final presentation of the school year. I presented to 600 youth in Port Coquitlam. I stood there, on my day off, in my regular clothes. None of my presentations ever spoke about police work nor did I promote any agency. The only thing I said in a presentation, is that I achieved my dream to become a Police Officer, and I showed the youth my badge. That's it. The presentations were about my story and that of Jamie's. It hadn't anything to do with policing at all. After the presentation, I met with several youth as I always do to answer questions or shake hands.

It was now the summer of 2013 and I rarely had presentations during this time, unless it was for a Community group or Corporate event. I used my days off to rest and work on the program development.

In early July, 2013, I was asked to come to the Deputy Chief's office for a meeting. I had suspected the meeting was being arranged to address the possibility of allowing me additional time through the year to do presentations, as I had requested in writing a few weeks prior. The RCMP has a policy related to supporting community relations that are in the best interest of the public. The RCMP can provide up to two weeks off per year to help promote that support. I had submitted a request and thought they wanted to address this. I was wrong.

The meeting started out well with the Chief and my

Inspector telling me how much they supported my work and such. I was then handed a five-page document which was from the Regional Ethics Officer. This was a person that I had never heard of, met or even spoken to in the past. The document was all about my program and what I was doing.

As I read the document, I realized it was an 'ethics complaint' that had been filed against me for my work with Bullying Ends Here. The document went on to say, 'the initial purpose of the website was to solicit funds on the site to offset his presentation travel costs'. The implication was that I had a second salary. This is absolutely false as the website was initially set up to be able to provide the support and resources needed to give the youth after a presentation along with contact information to be able to reach me. The addition of the page to donate was only added after the program became a charity and I wasn't working under the B.C. RCMP umbrella.

The document also said, 'Cst. MILMINE must be fully aware of the organizational risks and that he cannot be a free agent on his own time if he is representing the RCMP'. I never represented the RCMP directly while doing presentations. I never stated I was an RCMP officer, in fact. Any references on the website to my employer were direct links to the media clips that the RCMP had in fact set up for me and fully supported at the time. The photos and mention of the RCMP were public articles on television or in the newspaper.

The accusation that troubled me the most was, 'The Bullying Ends Here campaign is in direct competition with youth strategy programs that are delivered by Crime Prevention Services. The WITS program, for example, is supported by the RCMP nationally and brings together schools, families and communities to create responsive environments that help children deal with bullying and peer victimization.' I was stunned that anyone would state that there is a competition out there for trying to help youth. The WITS program is for grades kindergarten through grade six. Bullying Ends Here is only for grades six and above and is a story of resilience and the need for compassion. There is nothing about the Bullying Ends Here program that would compete with any other program in existence.

I was simply stunned as I sat there glancing at this document. I told my two superiors that no one had ever consulted with me regarding this document and that many of the points listed were either incorrect or completely false. I had no words to explain my confusion about how I created a program that the RCMP embraced and fully supported and then, when I decided that I wanted to go back to working as a first responder, made me the target of an ethics complaint.

I asked my superiors what I should do and they suggested that I put a rebuttal together and submit requesting permission from the RCMP to continue my work. I agreed to do the rebuttal but asked why I would need permission to continue as I would have thought that the permission was automatic since they had just supported me for six months doing the exact same thing that I had just completed. Since they supported me before, why would that change? I was told to; 'tow the line' and to 'work with them and not against them'. I was fuming inside but very calm and polite on the outside. I sat down for several days poring over the ethics complaint and put together my rebuttal. It was forty-six pages long and included quotes from the youth, teachers and over a dozen letters of support from various RCMP Inspectors across the Country who wanted to share their thoughts. I included news articles and also three pages of direct responses to the points listed in the original complaint.

I got a response a day later asking me to cut the document down as I could not expect anyone to read forty-six pages. I reduced it to around fifteen and was again told to reduce. This time I was told to use the template for outside business interests on the RCMP server. I tried to argue that what I was doing was not an outside business interest as I was not being paid in any way shape or form and was not representing the RCMP. Any connection made to my employer was not done by me during a presentation. The template they wanted me to fill out would not allow me to address the errors in the ethics complaint. I was not allowed to argue this point any further. I was again told to 'tow the line'.

I filled out the form and waited. During this time, I spoke to our Staff Relations Representative (SRR) as the RCMP does not have a union. I met with my SRR and went over the details of what was going on and for advice and direction. He told me to just keep doing what I was doing as I wasn't doing anything wrong and that someone would see the error that was taking place. I knew that what was happening wasn't because of the 'RCMP'. Rather, it was because of a couple of people that had very loud voices; voices that I could never defeat. My SRR figured that eventually someone higher up would see that this complaint was never about Bullying Ends Here, rather, it was about someone's ego and that I had upset people for not doing another year's secondment.

I spoke weekly with my SRR and was always advised to just keep doing the program. I had my direct supervisors, my colleagues and other RCMP staff attend presentations once the new school year started in September so that they could see for themselves what I was doing. Whenever anyone saw the program, they were puzzled as to why the complaint was issued and what the big deal was about. I had everyone's support.

In the fall of 2013, is when my request was forwarded to be reviewed by the Human Resources Officer for B.C. I was getting a few emails asking for clarification on accounting practices and such. I explained that not a single dollar had been donated to the charity and that the fiscal year for the Charity ended on December 31st. I also explained that the Charity was only in its first few months of operation so no filings had taken place yet. They wanted to know who would be doing the accounting for us.

I explained that, as a Charity, we were still working on that but would certainly share the name once the Board of Directors had decided on an accounting firm.

I was then directed to get a business licence from the city of Surrey. I outlined how the charity is not a business and that no funds were being made or donated. I explained how the charity was registered for the Country and not for the city of Surrey. At this point I knew that things weren't going well because I was told by my Inspector very firmly that I was to 'stop nit-picking' and that there was going to come a time that I would have to decide whether I still wanted to be an RCMP Officer and stop doing Bullying Ends Here or keep doing Bullying Ends Here but stop being an RCMP Officer.

I knew then that I was in a very difficult situation. The SRR was not getting anywhere with support nor was I getting anywhere with trying to have a reasonable discussion with my superiors. No one wanted to talk about the program or find out what precautions were being taken to safe-guard against any issues moving forward.

I remember distinctly on two separate occasions having senior members of staff saying to me, 'What happens when that fourteen year old boy makes an allegation against you?' Of course the first thing that crossed my mind is asking myself why does that scenario have to be a boy, the second being how do two men ask me the exact same question and why isn't anyone simply asking what I am doing to protect myself.

Pretty simple as far as I was concerned since I had been

doing the program for almost two years at that point with no issues or complaints. Certainly no allegations. If they had asked or listened to me, they would know that everything I do is by email and that I never meet anyone outside of the presentation or speak on the phone. There is no room for allegations. Even if one were to come forward then, well, they are the Police and could investigate it just like any other complaint that comes in.

Knowing that my time with the RCMP was nearing a point where I would have to choose between the charity or my career, I began to look at other options. I had just gone to Calgary for a week of presentations and was amazed at how so many Calgary Police Officers, both junior and senior, came out to see the presentation. I would guess that at least fifty had come out in total that week. I started to meet several key individuals within the Calgary Police Services and research what it was like to work in Calgary. I was really impressed the way I was treated and welcomed to the city overall. The people were friendly, the Police were well received by the public and the Calgary Police Service was well recognized across the Country. I spoke to their Human Resources department and began to learn what was required of me to consider a switch and the timelines we would be working with. I was also proactive in sharing what was happening with the RCMP and the challenges I was having. There were no secrets.

By the time March, 2014 came along, my stress was high and my ability to focus was difficult. It was a really tough situation to be in. I was fortunate enough to have achieved my dream because the RCMP believed in me but now I was in this terrible predicament with my job in jeopardy. I was clearly doing well with two Police Officer of the Year award nominations and top marks during my annual assessments. On my days off I was sharing my story and saving lives.

On March 11, 2014 I was called into the office one last time. I was in the room with my Inspector, the Superintendent and my Corporal. I knew exactly where the discussion was going to go but I wanted to hear them out. I was hoping for a last minute miracle. The discussion started out with the typical happy banter and how proud they were of me for the work I was doing. I listened intently and patiently while I was told that I should have stopped doing the program months ago while I waited for the approval to come through from the Human Resources Officer and how I was letting many people down. I was then handed a two page document. For lack of better words, it was a 'cease and desist' order.

This document went on to say that I had failed to respond to multiple requests and therefore my request for 'secondary employment' had been closed. I was told that I had not provided the documentation to confirm that I had a City of Surrey business license. This was confusing as well since I had spoken directly about this by email and during phone conversations with my Inspector on how the City of Surrey would not issue me a license as I am not a business and do not operate solely out of the city. I had this in writing and was told to 'hang onto it'. The requirements they insisted upon were impossible for me to achieve.

The final part of the document stated that I was not to do anything further with the program 'through the website, speaking or promotional activities associated to Bullying Ends Here' until the request for secondary employment had been reopened and approved. I explained that the requests being made were impossible and I was being set up to fail. I also asked how long might it take for the approval to come forward should I be able to meet these demands. I was told it might take six weeks or it could take six months.

I sat back in my chair, I looked at everyone directly and I

said, 'I am a damn good cop. When I leave here today, I am going home and I am going to respond to the emails I have received from youth today. I am going to continue to do the program as I have scheduled to date. We are all adults in this room and I am telling you that I am going to disobey your direct orders to stop so what is the next step'?

The Superintendent looked at me, while twiddling his pen between his fingers, and said, 'Tad, please don't put me in a position to have to discipline you'. Discipline me, I thought? For what? I looked back at him and said, 'I have been nominated for awards for my police work. On my days off I save lives. I cannot continue to work for an organization that does not realize that there are is more then one way to resolve an issue, bullying included. I am not doing anything wrong and for this reason, I quit'.

I left the room and went up to the Human Resources office to turn in my badge and sign the paperwork. I also called the Calgary Police Service and updated them on what had just happened. I went home and sat on my couch and was afraid. I stood up for what was right. I wasn't doing anything wrong and I knew that. My future was now uncertain and the badge that I had poured my heart and soul into, was being handed back.

I still don't know to this day, what went wrong. I don't know why someone wouldn't just sit down and discuss the situation with me. I don't know why it ended the way it did. I am grateful for the opportunity to wear the red serge, to work with some incredible people and to be inspired the way I was. I was sad to say goodbye but I knew that my time with the RCMP was over.

I know that the RCMP is a great organization and that they hadn't done me wrong. It was just a couple of people that did not like what I was doing and they wanted to have full control while I refused. My standing up to them might have been one of the riskiest things I had done in a long time but, as it turns out, it was the best decision I could have made.

The last part that I had to sort out was to do with the media as they were present everywhere I went to report on the program locally. Each time there as an assumption that I was an RCMP Officer which would no longer be accurate. I had to make a decision as to how best to go about this. I didn't want the story to go on and on for months in the media everywhere I went and I also didn't want this to be controversial. I decided to go public and get it all over with in one day. This would be best for the RCMP and the program as well. There was no avoiding the story getting out in the media, as anytime I would correct them about being with the Calgary Police Service the next question would be, 'Why the switch' and I wasn't going to lie.

When my story hit the media, I was awakened by my phone vibrating like crazy the next morning, March 13, 2014. The story had been picked up Nationally and I had media calling non-stop. I did interview after interview. I tried my best to keep it simple while not lying either. I felt like I was forced out of the RCMP. I had a choice to either quit the RCMP or quit Bullying Ends Here. The choice was mine and I chose to quit the RCMP. I had no guarantees on being accepted into the Calgary Police Service. I received hundreds of emails of support. I also received three negative emails.

On top of the media storm, I had two very mean spirited Facebook messages from 'friends' who felt that I was wrong in going to the media and speaking up.

On April 1st, 2014, I was sworn in as a Constable with the Calgary Police Service. I bought a house in Calgary and another chapter in my life was about to begin.

Ottawa

My second time in Ottawa was October, 2013, to be the guest of the Hubley family at an annual fundraiser created after Jamie passed away to raise funds for youth mental health. It's called the Kaleidoscope of Hope. I was honoured to have been invited and to be able to spend more time with Jamie's family. Allan had mentioned that he might say a few words about me while he spoke. He was the Honourable Co-Chair, along with Laureen Harper (wife of the former Prime Minister) and was due to speak first at the event.

It was all a bit of a blur but I remember Allan asking me to come up on stage and to accept the first ever award from the Kaleidoscope of Hope in recognition of my efforts to end bullying. I was then asked to tell some of my own story. I'm glad that I am not shy! I shared as much as I could while keeping it as short as possible. The crowd was very appreciative as I received multiple standing ovations throughout my unexpected speech.

Once this was done, there was the grand prize draw for a trip for two to Jamaica at a luxurious spa. Anyone who bought a key, could see if it would open the 'door to paradise,' and if the key opened the door, that person won. I had purchased a key but didn't get up to check it as I was sitting beside Mrs. Harper and we were deep in discussion. When I did pull my key out of my pocket, there was an audible gasp in the room as word spread quickly that I had a key and everyone knew that no one had won the grand prize yet. As the audience had just learned about my efforts while I spoke on stage, and how I did all of this on my own time and, at the time, at my own expense, you could feel the anticipation in the air.

Sure enough, I got up and walked to the door, inserted the key and the key worked. I won! I had never won a single dollar in my life! I just looked up and whispered, 'Thank you, Jamie'. Everyone was so excited. That was one of the most incredible nights. I should also add that I returned to this event in October, 2015. Just prior to attending the venue, I put a toonie into the vending machine for a Diet Coke at my hotel and, sure enough, a bottle comes out with 'Jamie' written on it. There is clearly a young man up above watching over me!

Many months prior to my departure from the RCMP, I had met a Canadian Senator from Ottawa while in Vancouver who had read about me in the newspaper and wanted to meet. During this visit, she mentioned that she wanted to have my efforts recognized in the Canadian Senate. As it turned out, this honour would take place, March 24th, 2014 only days after I left the RCMP. There were no words to describe how incredible this recognition was. I humbly accepted and asked if I could bring a Guest with me. I wanted to bring a young man along whole the program had helped a year prior and that his family and I had become close. The Senator gladly accepted and was even kind enough to write him into my recognition speech to acknowledge some of the amazing work he was doing in his own high school.

We arrived in Ottawa, March, 23rd, and met with Senator Jaffer in her office to go over the details of what was to transpire the next day. Senator Jaffer had also arranged for me to meet another Senator along with receiving a private tour of the Parliament Buildings. We sat and chatted over dinner and discussed the amazing work that Bullying Ends Here was doing.

The youth that I took with me, Austin, and I could barely sleep that night. We were so excited and anxious about the next day and all of the exciting unknowns. It was Austin's first time in Ottawa as well. We woke up early and headed right next door to the Parliament buildings to meet our contact. We were escorted inside the building and were given an incredible tour. We got to see so much more than the general public would. We even got to go inside the Opposition Lobby which is typically off limits to the average person.

We met some wonderful people and had the opportunity to introduce ourselves. Then it was time to hurry upstairs to the Senate itself, to the 'Red Chamber' where everything is red and vibrant. The history within that room, as I learned, was incredible.

Austin and I were ushered into the Governor General's box overlooking the Senate floor from the second level. Below and directly ahead was the Senate Speaker who stood and looked directly at me. I was asked to stand and that is when Senator Jaffer started to introduce me to the Senate members. It was a blur to be honest. Everyone was looking up, I felt so special and important. When the Senator was finished, all the Senators looked at me and started to shout, 'hear hear,' and cheer. I just wanted to take it all in, as it was a once in-a-lifetime opportunity for sure!

Again it was time to be ushered off and to the front atrium. This is where our soon to be Prime Minister, Justin Trudeau, was walking in the front doors. Austin didn't know who he was right away but Prime Minister Trudeau was so kind and caring. He came up to us, chatted and shook our hands. He had a big smile on his face and took his time speaking with us. I asked for a photo which he was happy to oblige. He then had to get his own day started and headed upstairs but a member of his team ran back and wanted a card on the program at the Prime Minister's request.

On one hand I was being forced to make tough decisions with the RCMP, but on the other, the Canadian Government recognized my work at the highest level. I think that is grounds for confusion for sure. It motivated me to do even more and reaffirmed that I had done nothing wrong. In fact I had done something right. I had stood up for what I believed and I had won.

Tad just prior to being recognized in the Canadian Senate

Austin, Prime Minister Justin Trudeau and Tad

Tad and Prime Minister Justin Trudeau

Laureen Harper, Allan Hubley and Tad

Calgary

While I was in Calgary giving a week's worth of presentations, I met one of the most amazing individuals, Constable Andy Buck. Andy was the Lesbian Gay Bisexual Transgendered (LGBT) Liaison Officer for the Calgary Police Service. His role is to be the link between the LGBT Community and the Calgary Police Service.

We had chatted briefly through email prior to my first visit to Calgary for presentations and he asked if he could attend one. The very first presentation I did was at a stunning school called Webber Academy. Andy and I met there for the first time. I did my presentation, met some amazing young people and then Andy and I spoke in greater detail about my program. He decided to attend every one of my presentations that week. He was the one to help introduce me to so many Calgary Police Service Members and Officers and invited many to the presentations in the coming days.

I credit Andy with my smooth transition to Calgary both on the work and personal side. He and his wife even helped me find my first house in the city.

Fast forward to April 1, 2014. I was shuttled down to the Calgary Courthouse and allowed to bring two guests or 'witnesses'. I wanted no one more than Andy and my incredible Human Resources Representative who had been my pillar of support through my challenging times at the end with the RCMP. It took less than forty-five seconds for the

Judge to walk into the room, ask me to swear that I will do the very best job that I can and, as quickly as he arrived, he was gone. I signed the paper and it was official.

Those eleven days between handing in my RCMP badge and officially resigning and then being sworn in with the Calgary Police Service were tough. There was much to do but also not having a badge itself was difficult. It's amazing how much something so small can mean to someone like myself. I was proud when I got my badge with the RCMP, but this day sure compares, if not exceeds those feelings.

My time in Calgary has been nothing short of a dream.

Everyone that I have met within the organization is a class act. I have been treated with dignity and respect. The Police Service has embraced Bullying Ends Here and has done much to help it get the recognition in Alberta that it needed. The Service recognizes that my program is another piece of the puzzle and has worked with me to ensure that precautions are in place as well. They have permitted me to continue doing exactly what I was prior to coming to Calgary. The only request they had was if I wouldn't mind telling everyone that I work for the Calgary Police Service. This is something I am so proud to say. I continue to keep the program and my work as separate as possible. I believe that it adds to the presentation when I can tell the audience that I am not paid to be there and that I do the program, and all presentations, on my own time. It just adds that additional element to how passionate I am at wanting to make a positive change in this world.

The work itself is the same of course. I still have to pinch myself from time to time realizing just how fortunate I really am. Everyday I get to go to work and do the job that I always dreamed of doing and then, on days off, I get to travel the country truly making a difference in people's lives. It's perfect!

Tad and Constable Andy Buck in Calgary

Tad and Rick Hanson, Former Calgary Chief of Police

Brian Burke, Mayor Nenshi, Jon Cornish, Tad, Andy Buck, John Fennell at a Calgary Fundraising Gala

Tad, Allan Hubley, Rick Mercer and Wendy Hubley

Tad and Brian Burke (Burkie)

The Past Returns

In March, 2015, I met someone. I won't use his name here as the point isn't to speak about him, rather the experience overall. He and I met on social media while I was presenting in Vancouver, and hit it off right away. He lived in Vancouver and I was in Calgary. He decided that he would move to Calgary with me to see where the relationship might go. This was all new to me but I sure loved it. I had never lived with someone before nor shared my bed with anyone. Almost as soon as he moved in, we were off for a three and a half week tour of Ontario, Nova Scotia, New Brunswick and Prince Edward Island giving presentations.

Talk about a good way to see if relationships are meant to be or not. From hotel to hotel, driving for hours every day, we stuck it out. In fact, it was great. Having someone to travel with was also new to me but something that I cherished. I officially had a boyfriend.

While in Ontario, we were going to visit my Mom and Stepdad so I decided to take my boyfriend to the house with the basement. I remember I pointed at it and said, 'There it is'. I hadn't told him prior to pulling up that I was going to take him there. I had never taken anyone there for fear that it might not be a positive experience. The house is just as beautiful on the outside now as it was back then. There are new owners now but the house was up for sale. We just drove by and I continued to show my boyfriend around my old stomping grounds. We spent some quality time with Mom and I did my presentations in the area for a few days. On one of the last days in Ontario, we again went past the house.

For some reason, I decided to stop and get out of the car. I never said anything while my boyfriend followed by getting out as well. There were two people on the front porch of the house and they welcomed me on the steps having no idea who I was. I told them that I grew up in that home. I was so nervous that I neglected to introduce myself, or my boyfriend. Without hesitation, the woman asked if I wanted to see inside. I said, 'Sure, but you have to know that my memories of this home are not all that great'. She had a puzzled look on her face but was so welcoming at the same time. She smiled and said, 'Let's start with your bedroom.'

We walked in the front door, something I rarely ever did as a child, and stood in the front area. The house looked just the same on the inside as I had remembered.

I pointed directly above our heads to the upper level and said, 'That's where my bedroom was'. The woman and her husband just looked at me puzzled. I knew the look was to do with how small the room was being not really ideal for a bedroom. As we walked up the steps to the upper level, I shared stories of how the house once looked and the changes that have taken place over the years since I had left. The bathroom had been totally redone and looked amazing. Everything else looked the same overall.

I then asked to see the basement. Both of the home owners stopped and said, 'Oh no, that's our dungeon and we don't even allow our children down there'. I said, 'Well I need to tell you about that dungeon then'. We slowly walked down the steps from the upper level of the house to the main floor as I spoke about the basement the way that I remember it. It was easy for me to talk about my experiences which surprised me. I had never really thought that I would go back to that house but I think that having my boyfriend with me was the support I needed. He and I never spoke while going through the house, but having him there was all that I needed. He had seen dozens of presentations by that point and I am sure his mind was piecing it all together while doing the tour of the house.

As we got to the top of the stairs that lead to the basement, we stood outside that door that I was so afraid of many years ago. I could still see the two small holes where the lock once was. The marks had been painted over by this time but it was clear what they were from. I rubbed them and spoke of how that lock felt like a bank vault door to me. I shared how that door was always closed and how the top step was where my food would often sit. We opened the door and one step at a time walked to the basement.

I could feel the anxiety building and sweat begin to bead on my neck. I felt safe, however the same feelings from the past were coming back with each step I took. As we rounded the corner and went down the final few steps, the ones that my ankles could have been grabbed through, the first thing I noticed was that the walls were the same. The same crumbling cement, same colours and the same smell. That smell was the exact same as I remember. Nothing had changed.

As I got to the bottom step, something was different however. The ceiling was now lower and I had to duck while I walked around. This is not the way it was when I was there.

Clearly I had grown taller over the years. There were still only a few lightbulbs in the ceiling, the same window from the past was cemented over but two new windows were now visible to see through. The cement floor was the same chestnut brown colour. The new owners had the washer and dryer in the same spots as we had back then.

As I looked around, everything came flooding back.

I could almost hear the screams, like the walls had held them in and were slowly releasing them once again. I could envision my little area in the far back corner where I spent so many years. The basement was now only used for laundry and storage but I was seeing it like it was the last time I was there. Although we only spent a few minutes down there, I felt like the walls were beginning to close in on me, like they were going to move in on me in such a way that I could not get out once again. I knew that I had spent enough time down there and needed to leave. I was also concerned that my stories of the past might influence the positive memories the current family had of their home. I certainly didn't want that to happen.

As my boyfriend and I were about to leave, I told them that I was writing a book and it would contain more of what I went through. They were so kind to pro-actively send many photos of the basement to add and to help you see for yourself just what the basement looks like. I can never thank them enough for that day and what it meant to me.

My boyfriend and I would return to Calgary but the next couple of months showed that we weren't compatible with each other. He left with nothing more than a text message while I was doing a presentation. I was heartbroken. I never did respond to it as I knew that he needed space and had clearly spent a lot of time thinking about his departure. I knew there would be nothing I could say that would bring him back. I had my chance.

I have to admit that I crashed in such a way that I would never have fathomed. I felt alone, abandoned and unwanted. I felt lost even though we were only together for three months. I called my Mom and broke down in tears which is something I had never done before. Mom is the person that I would always turn to when I needed someone to talk to. She has always been there for me. She gave me her words of encouragement and I worked to fix my broken heart. I was experiencing something at the age of forty-one that I should have experienced at the age of fourteen. A part of me knew that my feelings were silly as I had so much more in life to be happy about but, on the other hand, I beat myself up for the things that I didn't do for him. It would take me months and months to get past this and several counselling sessions. Counselling was always something that helped me and I have no issues reaching out for help when I need it.

I still have nightmares where I am in that basement. I wake up in sweats, my breathing heavy and wondering where I am when I first awaken. I struggle letting people into my life to the point that I feel vulnerable. I struggle with self-confidence from time to time. I still like to be alone and I get very uncomfortable when people feel sad or alone. I have all of the same feelings now as I did when I was the boy in the basement. Although I struggle with those moments in my life, I battle each and every day knowing that things are improving and that I have a wonderful life.

It's not lost on me that I did this. I am where I am today because of hard work and determination. I achieved my dream of being a Police Officer because I believed in myself, I worked hard and I tried. I get help when I need it. I try not to hide my past because I finally understand that it wasn't my fault. I wrote this book not for me, but for you. I wanted to share my own experiences of pain, neglect, abuse and the struggles with mental illness to show that dreams can still come true and that the future can be as bright as you want it to be. I wanted to show you what I did to make that all happen.

It's too late to help Jamie and I, but it isn't too late to help those that need it most. This is why I am so passionate about trying to make this world a better place. Every day I commit to telling the world about a boy named Jamie, a promise I made to his family and that I continue to do each and every day.

At the end of each day now, I look in the mirror at myself and ask, 'Was I the very best person I could have been today?'. This is what helps me reflect on the things that I said, the things that I did and those that needed help that I didn't help. I challenge myself to be even better tomorrow and to make a difference. I promise myself that I will work harder to be someone's voice and maybe even be someone's hero.

When I think like that, I know that I am making a difference in people's lives and that I am not only changing lives, but saving them. This is how I know that Bullying Ends Here.

Although I don't know where this journey in life will take me, I am thankful to be in such a position to try and help others. I hope to continue spreading Jamie's message of acceptance and understanding for years to come. I hope to continue proving to others that they are never alone and that help is all around. On the personal side, I hope to continue healing and to one day feel what it is like to be truly loved. As I always say, 'life is what we choose to make it'. I truly believe this. Life is all about choices that we make as individuals. I hope that by reading my book, you are inspired to lead by example and that you see how one person really can make a real difference in this world. Perhaps that person is you!

What The Kids Are Telling Me

*O*n average each year I receive close to 10,000 emails from youth. In order to email me, one needs to go to the website (www.bullyingendshere.ca), click on 'Contact Tad', and then fill out the form. To me, this says a lot about the connection made with the youth during a presentation. Although the vast majority of these emails are a simple 'thank you', many others are sharing with me their thoughts and concerns. I want to share some of the general remarks and concerns they are yelling me.

1. <u>Afraid</u>: I can't tell you how many emails I have received where a young person has expressed their fear of telling their parent or guardian about being bullied. They believe that by telling you, they will upset you. A victim of bullying will already feel minimized and the world is against them. To then have you be upset on top of the emotional assaults/taunting/brutality of it all, is just too much to handle so they would rather hold it in.

2. <u>Your Reaction</u>: Youth are afraid of your reaction in two ways. The first being that you will be upset or angry as I mentioned above and the second is what you will do when they do tell you. The fact is, that by the time they are ready to share with you, they have been through some very traumatic experiences and likely struggling with self esteem and possibly with their own mental health.

3. Punishment: This is a big one. Youth tell me what they won't tell you because they think you will take their phones or computers away from them if they share with you about online bullying. I understand why they fear this as I know it is a common reaction for adults. To think you will solve the problem by saying 'just turn the phone off and the problem is fixed' is not accurate. We have to understand that turning the phone off doesn't address the problem at all. A part of bullying that we have to understand is that it isn't always about what is happening directly to the child; it can also be what is happening indirectly, which includes social media. To take the Internet away from the youth simply removes the youth from the activity taking place. When the youth returns to school or to their social circles, they will be unaware of what has happened which can magnify the circumstances. Instead of 'punishing' your child by removing the Internet, take the time to work together to learn about what is being said by the bully, ways to correct the behaviours of all involved and how to use the Internet responsibly. I speak more to this, along with other suggestions in the following chapters.

4. Making it Worse: More often than not when I ask a youth why they haven't told a trusted adult about bullying, their answer is that the adult will only 'make it worse'. They believe that you will instantly go into 'mother bear' mode and do what YOU believe is appropriate to fix the problem. The fact is that what you believe is appropriate, might actually do what the youth fear; make it worse. As adults, we always want to protect the most vulnerable. It's the way most people react. As difficult as it is however, sometimes we have to simply

listen and empower the youth to make the decisions. I speak more to this in the following chapters as well, but its most important that we work with the young person to come up with a plan together. The 'fix' to end bullying starts with you. To immediately think the school is the answer is skipping the most important step. Before we jump to conclusions or want to place blame, we have to listen. I call the steps **LISTEN**, **ASK**, **AGREE**, **ACT**. After you have **LISTENED** to the issues, ask how you can help. Work on a plan together and agree on the plan. Only after you both **AGREE** to the plan, do you **ACT** on it. Don't do anything outside of the agreed-to plan as this could betray a trust no matter how much you believe it will help. Always **ASK** before you **ACT**. This will reduce the chances of you making it worse.

5. <u>Won't Understand</u>: Remember that youth never think an adult will understand, about anything! This is where the communication piece comes into play. To tell someone that you understand is just words. We all know the value of words alone. We have to prove that we understand and if we don't understand, take the steps necessary to learn. I provide some great resources at the end of this book to help but oftentimes the expert is the youth themselves. Ask them to help you understand. Especially when it comes to social media, adults might struggle with the understanding for the need to have so many forms of communication. The least you can do is try to comprehend, and even if you can't, then accept that times have changed when it comes to communication.

Signs of Bullying to Look For

It is very important to grasp that each point below does not necessarily mean a child is being bullied. On their own, the signs of bullying may simply be a change with societal changes, but could also point to signs of something more sinister. The following are some general things to look for.

1. Changes: A change of behaviour in activities or social circles. Perhaps your child stops doing something that they have previously enjoyed such as sports or games. Maybe they don't want to be out with friends as much and prefer to be alone.

2. Low self-esteem: You notice your child just doesn't seem the same. They appear to be sad or more introverted than normal; a change that appears different from the regular mood changes you know your child to have.

3. Moods: Sudden change in moods from happy to sad or content to angry. Changes that seem to happen suddenly and with minimal provocation. Of course everyone goes through puberty at some point and this might be a cause, but so can bullying.

4. Doesn't want to go to School: Unexplained stomach aches or other excuses why a young person doesn't want to go to school. Granted not everyone likes school but a victim oftentimes will do all they can to avoid locations that bullying is taking place.

5. <u>Unexplained injuries</u>: When your child starts showing random injuries that can't be explained and are not typical from their previous behaviours.

6. <u>Difficulty Sleeping</u>: This might include nightmares or sleep patterns that have not taken place in the past.

7. <u>Fear of Social Media</u>: A sudden change with not wanting to look at their phones or laptops almost as though they are afraid of these items.

What To Do If
Your Child Wants To Talk

The following steps are a general guideline and work off the principles that I call **LAAA**. **LISTEN, ASK, AGREE** and **ACT**. Every situation is different from the next and these steps are not meant to be the only way to move forward. They should be used as a general reference only and used in conjunction with what the experts say as well.

Step 1. Sit down with the child in a calm, quiet and comfortable atmosphere. Turn all phones and televisions off. Create an environment where it is safe to share information and perhaps consider opening up about some of your own challenges growing up. Remember that to a child, an adult is pre-historic and will never understand. We have to show that we DO understand while recognizing that bullying is not the same as it was twenty years ago.

Step 2. Once the child is comfortable and starts to share information, simply **LISTEN**. Do not interrupt them. Let them vent. **LISTEN** intently and without emotion. This is arguably the most important part. NEVER show negative emotion. If you show the child that you are angry, upset or anything along those lines, they can interpret that as now they are letting you down and they will cease to share. Save the emotion until you are away from the child at all times.

Step 3. When the child is done sharing, **ASK** how this is making them feel. It's important to hear it from them and have them reflect on it.

Step 4. **ASK** the child how it is that you might be able to help. Again this is VERY important. We have to give the child back a sense of empowerment. Let the child try to come up with an answer. I get thousands of emails from youth who tell me that their parents don't listen to them and simply try to fix things without their involvement. They are very frustrated by this. Empower your child. They are the best person for this since they are the ones experiencing it.

Step 5. Come up with a plan together and **AGREE** to it based on what the child wants. NEVER do anything that won't meet their approval. This includes going to talk to teachers or school faculty. If you take action against your child's wishes and they find out, again, the trust is removed and you just might make it worse.

Next steps are ONLY IF THE CHILD APPROVES.

Step 6. **ACT**. Arrange a meeting with those at the school or where the bullying is taking place. Include your child in this as well. Don't go into the school pounding fists on the table demanding change. You have to help them as well with plans. Go to the proper level of support such as Teachers or Principals, in your situation, armed with information, names, incidents, and a plan on how you think it might be resolved also. Remember that bullying is not going to stop overnight. It is going to take time.

Step 7. Once a plan is made, set target dates and follow ups. Try to do this in writing to keep records.

Step 8. If the school is powerless to change things, try the next step up in the chain of authority. Never skip steps of authority as you are only going to upset those you already negotiated with as you may need them again, however, you ignored them. Everyone is human after all.

Always keep the child included and updated on anything you learn. Continue to keep that comfortable discussion going. As adults we are busy, we all know that, but this should be a priority and time set aside to talk.

Going to the media is an adult thought. This would never be the choosing of the child. I would never ever recommend going to the media as the bullying is already between youth and the media battle would be all about the adults, fighting each other in the public forum. There is nothing positive that can come to the child through this. If anything, the child will be left with shame and embarrassment which is an element to bullying that they are most likely feeling already.

I realize that as adults we tend to want to fix everything. It's how we are programmed. Bullying is not a simple issue and won't be resolved overnight. We have to break the situation down and include everyone involved to work on a plan to find a resolution. We hear many negative reports in the news about bullying that we get really protective and always assume the worst without really knowing what is going on because we skipped the part about listening to our child. As adults we need to be providing our children with the tools and skills necessary to resolve their issues while empowering them to do so on their own as best as possible.

If cyber-bullying is involved, learn about the programs and apps being used by the public and find the ways in which the bullies can be reported, blocked and removed. There are more tips on the following sites;

www.bullyingendshere.ca
www.needhelpnow.ca
www.kidshelpphone.ca
www.cybertip.ca

Testimonials

"…thank you for the great presentation that you gave our kids. I want you to know that you have affected many of the students and that your name has been used in my office many times over the past couple of weeks. The kids see you as a true role model that they can look up to."

TEACHER

"I wanted to send you an enormous Thank you!! You gave a presentation at my son's school yesterday. He talked to me about your presentation all the way home from school, but nothing more. This morning he went into the school and asked to have a private conversation with his Learning Coach and he "told" all. I received an amazing phone call shortly after….

PARENT

"Your presentation made a difference in our school. Within a week of the presentation a few students came forward to me about the bullying that had been happening to them for almost a year. The bullying was happening both online and in person. I wanted to let you know that the student who was bullying is now being dealt with and the kids who are bullied are feeling much more safe. Thank you for making such a difference in the lives of so many people."

HEALTH CARE PROFESSIONAL

"I appreciate you sharing your story with us today more than you could imagine. You've have completely opened my eyes and I've come to realize that there's always a light at the end of the tunnel. Thank you so much for coming today, I hope

that eventually everyone in Canada has the opportunity to experience your presentation because it unlike anything I had ever heard before. The message that you've shared with us is something I know will stick with me for ever. You give people like me hope for the future and I'll never be able to thank you enough do that. Today's presentation was something I'll never be able to forget."

STUDENT

"I just want to thank you so much for saving my life. Your presentation showed me that there is light at the end of the tunnel. Because of your presentation, I've opened up to adults and am now getting treatment for two eating disorders, self-harm, depression, anxiety, and PTSD. I also struggle with my sexuality, and your talk helped me see that everything will get better. Maybe not today, maybe not tomorrow, maybe not for a month, but one day. You are an amazing man. Keep doing what you do. I can't thank you enough."

STUDENT

"In one short hour you were able to accomplish what I have been trying to accomplish for many years!!!"

PARENT

"I have been a public educator for 34 years and as a school principal for 25 years. I must say that I have never observed a more powerful, compelling presentation than Bullying Ends Here."

PRINCIPAL

"Thank you so much. You've inspired me so much these past two days. I went to my counsellor at school and there was a positive change. Telling an adult has helped. Thank you. :)"

STUDENT

"Usually when (my son) comes home he says hi mom and we chat for a minute or two, he gives his one word answers, then he disappears to his room or the basement. However, today he came home so moved by your story. We talked for at least 10 minutes. He told me so much about your life and the hardships and how you have overcome so much. He talked about the young boy who was an ice skater who committed suicide. He talked about the moment you told the kids that you were gay and how their opinions of you didn't change. He really admires your courage and strength and your ability to share your story. This is my son, who rarely says more than 10 words, who just kept talking about you! I just thought you should know you are changing lives and you are making a difference in the world. Way to go Tad."

PARENT

"My son met you last year and subsequently contacted you. This contact was the beginning of an entirely new chapter for him. He was in a very sad place last year and I really didn't know how to help him. I am happy to report that he is doing very well—best start to a school year ever. He is involved, confident and happy. I can't thank you enough for being there for him—he really related to you and you treated him like an intelligent and mature friend, which made all of the difference."

PARENT

Hundreds more are listed on bullyingendshere.ca…

Tad Milmine

Tad Milmine is a Police Officer in Calgary, Alberta, Canada with the Calgary Police Service. As a child, Tad was confined to a basement for many years, terribly bullied at school, and struggled with mental illness for many years. He also struggled with his own sexual identity until the age of twenty five. In 2011, having read about the suicide of fifteen year old Jamie Hubley, Tad decided to do his part to help change the world for the better. Tad created the award winning charity, Bullying Ends Here.

Tad gives heart-felt presentations to hundreds of school across Canada, and around the world, each year and has shared his own story of resilience and inspiration to hundreds of thousands of youth and adults. Tad has been recognized in the Canadian Senate, awarded the distinguished 'Kaleidoscope of Hope' award in 2012. Tad's efforts has also been recognized by the Governments of British Columbia and Alberta. Tad has been featured on hundreds of programs and stories around the world. To top it all off, Tad is also a best-selling author and voice to thousands who have felt alone for so long. Tad dedicates all of his work, efforts and awards, to the memory of Jamie Hubley.

To learn more, get involved or donate to the charity, please visit www.bullyingendshere.ca.

Acknowledgements

I would like to take this opportunity to thank a few very important people in my life.

First of all, thanks to my Mom and Stepdad (Dad) who have been there to support and accept me. You are both so amazing and I am proud to call you my parents.

I would also like to thank my best friend, Andy Buck. You have been my rock since the first day I came to Calgary for a presentation. I would be remiss if I didn't thank the Senior Staff of the Calgary Police Service for believing in me and allowing me the opportunity to continue achieving my dream of being a Police Officer while continuing to help make this world a better place.

Thanks to all those who have believed in me an accepted me as your friend. Life simply wouldn't be what it is today without you in it. I am thankful to say that there are too many of you to thank individually.

Lastly, I want to thank the Hubley family, for welcoming me and allowing me to share their son's story with anyone who will listen. I truly hope that the positive changes coming from the presentations, and this book, bring them some form of comfort to know that lives are being saved.

Tad Milmine
April 2015, Calgary, Canada